Why Are We Here?

ECCLESIASTES FOR TEENS

LUKE DOCKERY

Copyright © 2022 Deeper Youth Ministry. All rights reserved. No portion of this publication may be reproduced or transmitted in any form by any means—except for use in teaching contexts or brief quotations in published reviews—without the prior written permission of the author.

Scripture quotations are from the ESV® Bible (The Holy Bible, English Standard Version®), copyright © 2001 by Crossway, a publishing ministry of Good News Publishers. Used by permission. All rights reserved. The ESV text may not be quoted in any publication made available to the public by a Creative Commons license. The ESV may not be translated in whole or in part into any other language. The Holy Bible, English Standard Version®, is adapted from the Revised Standard Version of the Bible, copyright Division of Christian Education of the National Council of the Churches of Christ in the U.S.A.

DEEPER YOUTH RESOURCES

--- CORE VALUES ---

CHRIST CENTERED

DISCIPLESHIP FOCUSED

INTERGENERATIONAL

INTELLECTUALLY CHALLENGING

DISCUSSION BASED

The central mission of Deeper Youth Ministry is **"Cultivating Lifelong Disciples of Jesus,"** and this task is the driving force behind our resources. Deeper Youth Resources are:

- **DISCIPLESHIP FOCUSED**: Our resources encourage students to embrace a self-denying lifestyle where following Jesus and and sharing Him with others are the foremost priorities of their lives.
- **CHRIST CENTERED**: Discipleship is inherently focused on Jesus. Our resources seek to point people to the person and work of Jesus Christ, as described and revealed in the pages of Scripture.
- **INTELLECTUALLY CHALLENGING**: Our resources seek to engage the intellect God created us with in order to see what the Bible has to say about the world's tough questions, and to learn why we believe what we do.
- **INTERGENERATIONAL:** Research has shown that one of the keys in helping young people create a lasting faiths for them to develop close relationships with older Christians who can model faith for them. Our resources seek to provide opportunities for those relationships to develop.
- **DISCUSSION BASED**: Teens who are brought up in the church spend a lot of time in Bible classes and listening to sermons, but studies show that almost all of them struggle to put their faith into their own words. Our resources provide frequent venues for discussion that enables students to practice doing exactly that.

WWW.DEEPERYOUTHMINISTRY.COM

WHY ARE WE HERE?
TABLE OF CONTENTS

Author's Preface	7
What's Life All About? *Series Introduction*	9
Getting Our Bearings *Introduction to Ecclesiastes*	11
What Do You Mean By "Meaningless"? *Ecclesiastes 1*	21
A Desperate Search for Meaning *Ecclesiastes 2*	33
The Seasons Of Life *Ecclesiastes 3*	41
Barriers To Joy *Ecclesiastes 4*	49
Enjoying God's Gifts *Ecclesiastes 5*	57
The Value Of Contentment *Ecclesiastes 6*	67

God Is In Control 73
Ecclesiastes 7

The Value And Limits Of Wisdom 85
Ecclesiastes 8

Death is Coming 93
Ecclesiastes 9

The Power of Foolishness 101
Ecclesiastes 10

Take a Chance 111
Ecclesiastes 11

The End of the Matter 119
Ecclesiastes 12

Bibliography 129

Image Credits 133

About the Author 135

AUTHOR'S PREFACE

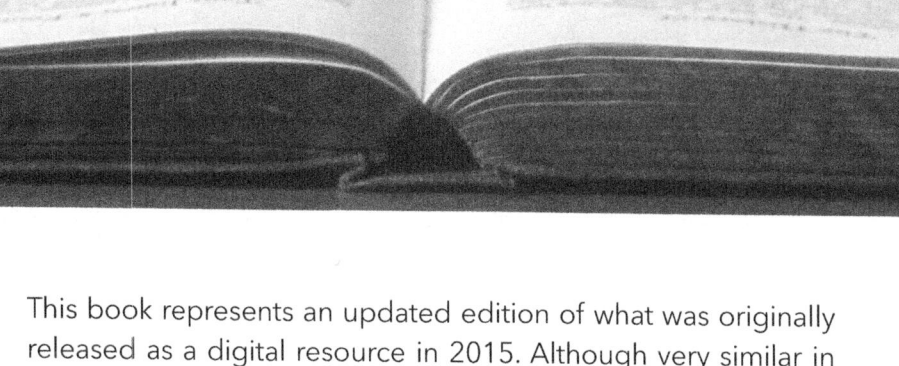

This book represents an updated edition of what was originally released as a digital resource in 2015. Although very similar in many respects to the original, this edition does contain typographical corrections as well as some theological nuancing and development as I have continued to study the book of Ecclesiastes.

It is my hope that this book will help you better understand and appreciate Ecclesiastes, which I believe to be as relevant in today's world as it was when it was first written.

May God bless us as we study His word and transform us into the likeness of His Son by the power of the Spirit.

Luke Dockery
August 2022

WHAT'S LIFE ALL ABOUT?
SERIES INTRODUCTION

Overview

The book of Ecclesiastes is part of the wisdom literature of the Old Testament and seeks to determine what is truly significant in life. It is a challenging and important book that deserves close examination.

This series will look at Ecclesiastes in detail in order to see what it has to teach people of faith about wisdom, our priorities, and what really matters in life.

Lesson Format

Each of our lessons are drawn from Ecclesiastes, and the biblical text is provided from the English Standard Version (ESV). It is recommended that you encourage your students to read the text as homework *before they come to class,* and then read it again together *in class*. This way, the text itself will be as familiar as possible and provide a better foundation for exposition and discussion.

Throughout the main body of the lesson, the text of Ecclesiastes is discussed in detail. In addition to teaching notes, discussion questions are provided throughout the lesson that give your students the opportunity to process what has been taught, verbalize what they have learned, and wrestle with applying the material to everyday life.

Each lesson also features several special sections:

- **THE POINT:** Each lesson begins by highlighting the overarching take-away from the lesson. This is the point that should be reinforced throughout the lesson.

- **DIVE IN:** All of the lessons begin with an activity or object lesson that serves to focus the attention of your students and get them thinking about the topic.

- **GO DEEPER:** Sprinkled throughout many (but not all) of the lessons, these optional sections provide more detailed background or technical information to help deepen your study. Depending on the age and maturity level of your students and the nature of the information provided, you might find this section to be incredibly valuable or something you would rather skip.

- **LIVE DEEPLY:** Each lesson ends with an exercise to connect what has been learned to real life, as we try to encourage students to live as disciples of Jesus. This section will consist of a variety of activities, but often, these activities will provide your students with the opportunity to interact with believers of other generations, whether Christians who are older than they are, parents, or even younger children.

GETTING OUR BEARINGS
INTRODUCTION TO ECCLESIASTES

The Point

In this lesson, we will introduce Ecclesiastes and provide an understanding of who may have written it, what kind of writing it is, and the purpose for which it was written.

Dive In: Famous Sayings Quiz

A lot of students won't know much (if anything) about the book of Ecclesiastes, but they may be familiar with several famous sayings that come from it. To introduce some of these sayings to your students, give them a quiz: pass out pencils and paper, have them number their papers 1-10, and for each saying you read aloud, have them write "yes" or "no" depending on whether or not they think the saying comes from Ecclesiastes. Afterwards, go over the correct answers, see how everyone did, and give a small prize to the winner.

1. *"To everything there is a season."* [**YES**; Ecc. 3.1]
2. *"Do unto others as you would have them do unto you."* [**NO**; Luke 6.31]
3. *"Two are better than one."* [**YES**; Ecc. 4.9]

4. *"A time to kill and a time to heal."* [**YES**; Ecc. 3.3]
5. *"Cleanliness is next to godliness."* [**NO**; Hebrew or Babylonian proverb]
6. *"Whatever your hand finds to do, do it with all your might."* [**YES**; Ecc. 9.10]
7. *"To thine own self be true."* [**NO**; *Hamlet,* by William Shakespeare]
8. *"There is nothing new under the sun."* [**YES**; Ecc. 1.9]
9. *"The Lord is my shepherd; I shall not want."* [**NO**; Psalm 23.1]
10. *"All men are created equal."* [**NO**; *The Declaration of Independence*]

Ecclesiastes 1.1-3

The words of the Preacher, the son of David, king in Jerusalem. Vanity of vanities, says the Preacher, vanity of vanities! All is vanity. What does man gain by all the toil at which he toils under the sun?

Background Information on Ecclesiastes

Before we launch into studying the text of Ecclesiastes in detail, it would be a good idea for us to first examine some important characteristics of the book: **author**, **genre**, **date**, and **purpose**.

AUTHOR

Who wrote Ecclesiastes? The author doesn't give his name, but instead calls himself *Qoheleth* (pronounced *ko-hell-it*), a Hebrew word meaning "gatherer" (*Ecclesiastes* is the Greek form of the Hebrew word *Qoheleth*).

But what is Qoheleth gathering? He could be gathering people, which is why some English translations (like the ESV) translate the word as "preacher" (in a sense, preachers gather people together to speak to them). Yet, Ecclesiastes doesn't really

Go Deeper: Hebrew vs. English

Most of the Old Testament, including Ecclesiastes, was written in Hebrew. Unlike English, Hebrew is written from right to left. See the image to the right to compare the word *Qoheleth* in Hebrew and English.

קֹהֶלֶת

qoheleth

contain any sermons.[1] He could be gathering observations and proverbs about wisdom to share with others, which is why the word is also translated as "teacher" (as in the NIV).[2] So, the author of Ecclesiastes is *Qoheleth,* the "Preacher" or "Teacher", depending on which translation you happen to be using.

Still, though, there is a longstanding tradition that this Teacher is none other than King Solomon, and that he wrote Ecclesiastes in his old age.[3] Indeed, there are a few clues in the text that point to this possibility: he is referred to as "The son of David, king in Jerusalem" (Ecclesiastes 1.1,12), and he speaks of his unsurpassed wisdom (1.16), unparalleled works (2.5-7), unequaled wealth (2.7-8), and unimaginable harem of women (2.8).

KING SOLOMON

---

[1] Roland E. Murphy, *The Tree of Life: An Exploration of Biblical Wisdom Literature* (Grand Rapids, MI: Eerdmans, 2002), 49.

[2] Phillip McMillion, *Wisdom Literature Class Lecture Notes* (Memphis: Harding University Graduate School of Religion, Fall 2010).

[3] F.C. Cook, ed., *Proverbs–Ezekiel,* The Bible Commentary (Grand Rapids, MI: Baker Book House, 1962), 87: "This book is placed, in the most ancient Jewish and Christian lists, between the other two Books (Proverbs and Song of Solomon) attributed to Solomon, and the constant tradition of the Jewish and Christian churches has handed down Solomon without question as author."

DISCUSS: What do you know about Solomon? *(He was a king in Jerusalem, he was the son of David, he was known for his wise and understanding heart, he amassed great wealth, accomplished many things, had many wives and concubines.)*

All of this seems to suggest that the Teacher certainly *could* be Solomon, but there are arguments *against* Solomon being the author as well:

- The Teacher seems to speak of his reign in the past tense (1.12), while we know that Solomon was king until the day he died.[4]
- He mentions "all who were over Jerusalem" before him (1.16), but only two kings preceded Solomon on the throne of Israel.[5]
- The teacher quits using the image of kingship in chapter two, and from that point on, is critical of the king when he mentions him (4.13-16, 5.8-9, 8.2-4, 10.4-7, 10.16). Would Solomon be so critical of himself?[6]
- The Hebrew used in Ecclesiastes is generally considered to be from a later time period than that of Solomon.

DISCUSS:

- **Do you think Solomon wrote Ecclesiastes, or someone else?**
- **Does it matter whether or not it was Solomon?**
- **When does biblical authorship matter?**

---

[4] Devin Swindle, "What Dreams Are You Chasing?," in *Deeper Faith: 2014 Deeper Youth Conference*, ed. Luke Dockery and Jake Greer (Fayetteville, AR: Deeper Youth Ministry, 2014), 203.

[5] Swindle, 203.

[6] Ibid.; Murphy, 49; Dave L. Bland, *Proverbs, Ecclesiastes, & Song of Songs*, The College Press NIV Commentary (Joplin, MO: College Press Publishing Company, 2002), 293.

When a book of the Bible identifies a specific person as its author, we need to take that claim very seriously, but in this case, since Ecclesiastes doesn't specifically claim that Solomon is the author, other options seem possible. Since the author refers to himself as the Teacher, that's how we'll refer to him throughout this book. It does seem clear, however, that the Teacher uses a kingly/Solomonic persona in order to share the lessons that he's trying to teach; we'll discuss that further in the next section.

It is also worth pointing out that there appears to be an editor who was involved in compiling the final text of Ecclesiastes, as there are multiple editorial comments where the Teacher is referred to in the third person (1.1, 7.27, 12.9-10). Scholars disagree about how to interpret the relationship between this final editor and the Teacher; we will discuss that relationship more in a later chapter.[7]

Of course, we should also emphasize that, regardless of who the human author is, all Scripture is God-breathed (2 Timothy 3.16-17). As part of God's inspired word, Ecclesiastes has some important lessons to tell us about life regardless of which human God inspired to write it.

GENRE

The term genre refers to a specific type of literature.

DISCUSS: What are some different genres that we find in the Bible? *(Gospels, History, Epistles, Law, Poetry, Prophecy, Apocalypse, etc.)*

In a general sense, Ecclesiastes is usually grouped with the other Wisdom Literature of the Bible (Job and Proverbs in

---
[7] See the Go Deeper section on p. 126-27, "Who Wrote the End of Ecclesiastes?"

particular, and occasionally Psalms and Song of Songs), and certainly Ecclesiastes is concerned with wisdom.

More specifically, Ecclesiastes has much in common with a type of ancient writing called Royal Instruction, a first-person narrative where a dead or dying king gives instructions to the leader who is going to follow him. This form was often used in a time of instability to help support a new king. The writer would speak as the dead king, recount the deeds of the previous ruler, and would then give instructions on how to achieve stability and order and how to govern wisely.

We can see some parallels here with Ecclesiastes, where a past ruler speaks from his experience in order to guide later generations. So, it is possible that Ecclesiastes was a type of Royal Instruction writing with some proverbs included as well.

This perhaps helps us deal with some of our earlier questions about authorship: Ecclesiastes could have been written long after the time of Solomon, but could be using Solomon as a well-known and respected character from the past. This would not be an attempt by the writer to deceive anyone, as he would be using a form and style well known to his audience (i.e., readers would realize that it was not written by Solomon but rather by someone adopting his persona).[8]

Consider a more modern example: in the late 1930s and early 1940s before the United States entered World War II, there was a significant debate in this country about whether or not Americans should be involved in what was largely considered to be a European war. Imagine if someone were to write a letter to the editor in the newspaper advising the country to avoid entanglements in foreign affairs, especially those of Europe, and

---

[8] McMillion.

then signed the letter "George Washington".[9] No one would really believe that George Washington had written the letter, and no one would feel that they had been deceived or that the newspaper had lied to them; readers would understand that this was simply a way of writing to make a point.

None of this proves that this is what happened with Ecclesiastes, but the similarity between Ecclesiastes and other Royal Instruction writings at least makes this a possibility.

DATE

We really don't know when Ecclesiastes was written. If it was actually written by King Solomon, it would likely be late in his reign as king (930s BC). If it was written by someone else, it could be much later, maybe even after the Exile based on the development of Wisdom Literature and the style of Hebrew language it uses (540-300 BC).

---

[9] In Washington's Farewell Address as President of the United States, he advised those who came after him to seek to remain neutral in world conflicts and avoid foreign entanglements.

Purpose

Ecclesiastes is all about the search for the meaning and significance of life.[10] As the Teacher puts it in 1.3: *"What do people get for all their hard work under the sun?"* (NLT). This question is posed, I think, in frustration and desperation from the realization of 1.2: *"Vanity of vanities, says the Preacher, vanity of vanities! All is vanity."* Or, in the NIV: *"Meaningless! Meaningless! says the Teacher. "Utterly meaningless! Everything is meaningless."*

Everything is meaningless?! That sounds like a pretty low view of life! This idea of "meaningless" or "vanity" is very important to Ecclesiastes, and if we are going to understand what the Teacher is trying to say, we need to get a good handle on this word and what it means. That will be the focus of our next lesson.

> ### Live Deeply: Mature Christian Interview
>
> For this to work well, you need to have your students interview an older member of your church family **before** class. Have students ask their interviewee the following question and write down the responses:
>
> *What life advice would you give teenagers today?*
>
> As a class, share the different responses that the students have collected and then combine them to create an advice letter. This will serve at least two purposes: (1) It will

---

[10] Bland, 291, nicely captures the purpose of Ecclesiastes and compares it to other Old Testament books of Wisdom Literature: "When one enters into wisdom's world, one embarks on a journey. In the book of Proverbs, this journey leads a person to seek out the order by which creation and society live. In the book of Job, wisdom's journey leads one on a quest for the presence of God. In Ecclesiastes, the journey leads to the search for meaning in life."

help to illustrate **Royal Instruction** writing, where an older, wise person offers advice to those who are younger, and (2) Your class will glean a lot of practical life advice from older, mature Christians who have already walked in their shoes.

WHAT DO YOU MEAN BY "MEANINGLESS"?
ECCLESIASTES 1

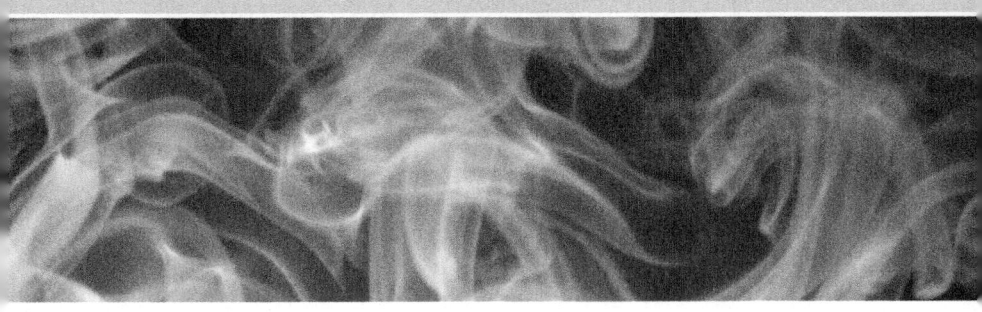

The Point

In this lesson, we will develop a good grasp of different possible meanings of the Hebrew word *hebel* and how it is important to understanding the book of Ecclesiastes.

Dive In: A "Case" Study

The Hebrew word *hebel* is very important in Ecclesiastes, but it is a word that has different meanings in different contexts.

To introduce this word study to your students, divide them into small groups and, after passing out pencils and paper, have them list as many possible meanings of the word "case" as possible. After a few minutes, have a representative from each group share all of their list and then generate a master list up on the board (some possible meanings are provided below).

POSSIBLE MEANINGS OF *CASE*

An Argument: "Make a case" for something

An Example: "This is a case of _____"

A Container: Pencil case or briefcase

A Lawsuit or Trial: "The OJ Simpson case"

An Instance of Disease: A case of pneumonia

A Crazy Person: "That guy is a nutcase!"

An Expression of Frustration: "Get off my case!"

A Form of Letters: Upper case and lower case letters

Ecclesiastes 1.1-11

The words of the Preacher, the son of David, king in Jerusalem. Vanity of vanities, says the Preacher, vanity of vanities! All is vanity. What does man gain by all the toil at which he toils under the sun?

A generation goes, and a generation comes, but the earth remains forever.

The sun rises, and the sun goes down, and hastens to the place where it rises.

The wind blows to the south and goes around to the north; around and around goes the wind, and on its circuits the wind returns.

All streams run to the sea, but the sea is not full; to the place where the streams flow, there they flow again.

All things are full of weariness; a man cannot utter it; the eye is not satisfied with seeing, nor the ear filled with hearing.

What has been is what will be, and what has been done is what will be done, and there is nothing new under the sun.

Is there a thing of which it is said, "See, this is new"?

It has been already in the ages before us.

There is no remembrance of former things, nor will there be any remembrance of later things yet to be among those who come after.

Looking Closer at "Vanity"

Discuss: Last time, we talked about the author, genre, date, and purpose of the book of Ecclesiastes. What do you remember from last week?

A big takeaway from last week is that Ecclesiastes was written by a wise teacher who is wanting to share his thoughts on what life is all about. In Ecclesiastes 1.3 he asks, *"What do people get for all their hard work under the sun?"*, and that question is asked, I believe, in frustration and desperation from his realization of 1.2: *"Vanity of vanities, says the Preacher, vanity of vanities! All is vanity."* Or, in the New International Version: *"Meaningless! Meaningless! says the Teacher. Utterly meaningless! Everything is meaningless."*

This serves as a good transition to this week's discussion on Ecclesiastes 1 and the meaning of the word that our English Bibles generally translate as "vanity" or "meaningless".

In Hebrew, that word is *hebel* (pronounced heh-vul) (הבל), and it represents an important theme in the book of Ecclesiastes. In fact, *hebel* occurs 38 times in Ecclesiastes, more than the rest of the Old Testament combined.[11] Literally, the word *hebel* means "breath", and when used as a metaphor (after all, it doesn't really make literal sense to say "Everything is breath!"), there are a few different possibilities of how it should be translated.

Before we look at those different possible translations, though, we need to notice that in Ecclesiastes 12.8, there is a repetition of what occurs in 1.2: *"Vanity of vanities, says the Preacher. All is vanity."* In biblical studies, this is called an *inclusio*, "a phrase or idea that brackets a work when it is found at the opening

---

[11] Bland, 294.

and closing."[12] In literature studies, this might be referred to as framing. Basically, the frame should help us to interpret everything else that occurs inside the frame. That means that this idea of *hebel* or "vanity" is going to be very important to our interpretation of Ecclesiastes.

DISCUSS:

- What other words do your Bibles use to translate this idea?
- When you hear the word "vanity", what are some different ideas you associate with that word?

We will look at this closely, because how we interpret the *hebel* frame will greatly influence how we interpret the rest of Ecclesiastes. Since the word *hebel* can have many different meanings depending on the context (like the word "case" from our opening activity), we need to work to get at the real meaning of this word in context in order to understand what the Teacher is really trying to say.

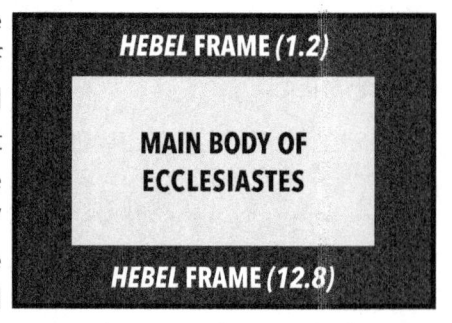

HEBEL FRAME (1.2)

MAIN BODY OF ECCLESIASTES

HEBEL FRAME (12.8)

POSSIBLE MEANINGS OF HEBEL

Similar to the word "case", the Hebrew word *hebel* has a range of possible meanings, and any of these meanings can be legitimate interpretations of *hebel* depending on the context.[13]

(To help your students keep these different possibilities separate in their minds, you might consider writing them on

---

[12] McMillion.

[13] The discussion and summary of the different possible interpretations that are presented here come largely from Bland, 294-98, and McMillion.

the board along with different emojis to emphasize how optimistic/pessimistic they are.)

Vanity: This is the traditional understanding and is what is found in most English translations. This interpretation conveys the sense of meaninglessness or emptiness, and gives Ecclesiastes a pretty pessimistic and negative outlook on life. If everything is meaningless, then what are we doing here?

Absurdity: According to this perspective, Ecclesiastes argues that there *should* be some meaning to life, but, unfortunately, there just isn't. Life is absurd, and this is the problem the Teacher is writing about. This means that life is unreasonable or irrational, deprives human action of meaning, and really undermines morality, because there is no point or reason to being good people. This is an extremely negative view.[14]

Mystery: This interpretation might go well with the idea of "breath" (remember, *hebel* literally means "breath") in the sense of being hard to grasp: life is so inconsistent, unpredictable, and mysterious that, at least sometimes, it simply cannot be understood. The idea that life is incomprehensible is better than life being meaningless or absurd, but it still leaves us in a frustrating place: life may have meaning, but we struggle to know what it is.

Temporary: A fourth option interprets *hebel* as something that is fleeting, not lasting, or something that quickly fades away. This is, perhaps, a more positive interpretation than the other options. It's not that life is empty or meaningless; indeed, there are beautiful aspects of life that bring great joy, but ultimately, these things do not last.

So, which of these meanings best fits the context of

---

[14] William P. Brown, *Character In Crisis: A Fresh Approach to the Wisdom Literature of the Old Testament* (Grand Rapids, MI: Eerdmans, 1996), 131.

Ecclesiastes? Acknowledging that this is a very debated question, I still think we can arrive at some clarity. The first two options, **vanity** and **absurdity**—both of which question whether or not there is any meaning to what we experience in life—are problematic, because the Teacher of Ecclesiastes does not see everything in the world as meaningless. In fact, in multiple places he recommends living in certain ways, which would make no sense if everything was meaningless.[15]

There is some textual support for the third possibility, that *hebel* means that life is **mysterious** and hard to figure out. Consider Ecclesiastes 8.14, where the Teacher reflects on the fact that sometimes tragedy befalls good people while bad people seem to flourish. Or Ecclesiastes 3.11, where he mentions that humans are unable to understand or discover what God has done throughout time.[16] Certainly, part of what *hebel* means is that there are aspects of life that are very difficult—if not impossible—to understand.

Finally, there is a lot of textual evidence within Ecclesiastes and also the rest of the Hebrew Bible that supports the interpretation of *hebel* as **temporary**:

- Isaiah 57.13: *hebel* is paralleled with "wind" (רוח), something transitory or quickly passing away.
- Job 7.16: Job doesn't want to live forever; his days are just *hebel* (this could easily be a reference to the shortness of life).
- Jeremiah 10.15, 51.18: *hebel* is translated "worthless", but with the clear idea of passing away.
- Psalm 39.5, 11, 78.33, 144.4: a breath that quickly passes away.
- Proverbs 31.30: is beauty worthless or bad, or is it just fleeting?

The idea of temporary or quickly passing would fit well in

---

[15] Bland, 295. See, for example, Ecclesiastes 2.24-26; 9.7-10.

[16] Ibid., 296.

hebel passages in Ecclesiastes as well:

- Ecclesiastes 6.12: "For who knows what is good for man while he lives the few days of his *hebel* life, which he passes like a shadow?"
- Also 3.19, 7.15, 9.9, 11.8: "vain" could be translated "brief" in each of these instances and fit the context well.

Taken together, it seems to me that *hebel* in Ecclesiastes conveys the idea that **life is both fleeting and hard to understand.**[17] In *The Message*, Eugene Peterson translates *hebel* with the English word "smoke", and I think that works quite well: smoke dissipates and does not last long, and it is something that cannot be grasped.[18]

Go Deeper: The Hebrew Superlative

In grammar, the **superlative** form is used to express the greatest or most of something. In English, we usually indicate the superlative by adding the suffix *-est* (big*gest*, friendli*est*) or the word "most" (most recent, most special).

Hebrew uses an idiom for the superlative, and "Vanity of Vanities" is an example of this (see also "Song of Songs" or "Holy of Holies"). So basically, by using the Hebrew superlative, the Teacher is saying that life is absolutely *hebel*. It couldn't be more impermanent or mysterious than it is.[19]

---

[17] Ibid., 297. BibleProject, "Ecclesiastes," directed by Jon Collins and Tim Mackie, June 10, 2016, 8:01, https://bibleproject.com/explore/video/ecclesiastes/.

[18] Eugene H. Peterson, *The Message: The Old Testament Wisdom Books* (Colorado Springs: Navpress, 1996). BibleProject, "The Book of Ecclesiastes: Wisdom Series," directed by Jon Collins and Tim Mackie, August 17, 2016, 6:41, https://bibleproject.com/explore/video/wisdom-ecclesiastes/, "Like smoke, life is confusing. It's disorienting and uncontrollable."

[19] Murphy, 53.

This greatly impacts how we interpret Ecclesiastes: it's not that everything in life is sad, empty, or meaningless. On the contrary, there are multiple places in Ecclesiastes that emphasize the joy that comes from appreciating God's gifts and the good things in life.[20] Ultimately, though, even these good things—whether beauty, wisdom, or relationships—do not last and will pass away, and they are also balanced by difficult circumstances in life that are simply beyond our understanding.

Acknowledging that life is *hebel* allows us to accept that life is largely out of our control and frees us to trust God and gratefully enjoy the gifts He bestows upon us, despite the fact that we remain puzzled by the mysterious nature of life.[21]

DISCUSS:

- Which of these four possible interpretations of *hebel* makes the most sense to you?
- Does it seem to you that life is like a breath in the sense that it passes by quickly and does not last long?
- Is life mysterious?
- Read James 4.13-14; what do these verses have to do with our discussion on *hebel*?

Go Deeper: *Hebel* and *Abel*

In this lesson, we have been studying the Hebrew word *hebel* (הבל) which literally means "breath", and have suggested that, in Ecclesiastes, it conveys the meanings of both "brief" and "mysterious."

In Genesis 4, we read of Adam and Eve's two sons, Cain

---

[20] See R.N. Whybray, "Qoheleth, Preacher of Joy," *JSOT* 23 (1982): 87-98.

[21] BibleProject, "Ecclesiastes."

and Abel (הבל). That's right: Abel's name comes from the same word, *hebel*, which we have been studying in this lesson.

Especially in the Hebrew Bible (Old Testament), names often reveal some part of a person's character. For example, Abraham means "father of a multitude", which makes perfect sense for the man who was the father of the Hebrew people.

In the same way, "breath" or "brief" was a fitting name for Abel; he embodied the fact that life is temporary, and, in many ways, hard to understand, as, despite his righteous living (or, actually *because* of it!), he was killed by his brother in a fit of jealous rage.[22]

Once we have a grasp of *hebel*, the rest of Ecclesiastes 1 is pretty straightforward. In 1.3, the Teacher asks the big question: What is the point? What is the gain or benefit of all the work we do? And the Teacher is going to begin the process of answering his own question, which he will continue to do for the rest of the book.

In 1.4-11, the Teacher illustrates the cycle of life (generations of people come and go, the sun rises and sets, the wind blows all over, etc.), and as part of that cycle, the **impermanence** of life. This reminds us of the fleeting aspect of *hebel*.

Also, in 1.9-10 the Teacher introduces the idea that "there is nothing new under the sun". This idea may assault us somewhat as modern Americans: with all of our technological innovations, we like to think that we're doing something new

---

[22] Russell L. Meek, "The Meaning of הבל in Qohelet: An Intertextual Suggestion," in *The Words of the Wise Are like Goads: Engaging Qohelet in the 21st Century*, ed. Mark J. Boda, Tremper Longman III, and Cristian G. Rata (Winona Lake, IN: Eisenbrauns, 2013), 252-54.

and impressive, but the Teacher seems to disagree.

DISCUSS: What do you think the Teacher is trying to say here?

I think 1.11 is also a slap in the face that should humble us a little bit. We like to think that we are important and that we make a big impact, but realistically, what we do will be forgotten soon after we are gone; very few people alter world history in such a way that they are remembered for long.

That doesn't mean that our lives are unimportant or that we should give up, but it should cause us to question our motives: if you do what you do in order to impress others so that they will remember how great you are, you are being incredibly foolish, because no one will![23]

Ecclesiastes 1.12-18

I the Preacher have been king over Israel in Jerusalem. And I applied my heart to seek and to search out by wisdom all that is done under heaven. It is an unhappy business that God has given to the children of man to be busy with. I have seen everything that is done under the sun, and behold, all is vanity, a striving after wind.

What is crooked cannot be made straight, and what is lacking cannot be counted.

I said in my heart, "I have acquired great wisdom, surpassing all who were over Jerusalem before me, and my heart has had great experience of wisdom and knowledge." And I applied my heart to know wisdom and to know madness and folly. I perceived that this also is but a striving after wind.

For in much wisdom is much vexation, and he who increases knowledge increases sorrow.

---

[23] Brown, 149.

The first chapter of Ecclesiastes ends with somewhat of a summary in 1.12-18. Life is fleeting and mysterious. There are wrongs that cannot be righted and empty holes that cannot be filled in this earthly life.

Seeking wisdom is good (in fact, that's what the book of Proverbs is all about), but ultimately, earthly wisdom cannot answer all of life's questions. In fact, 1.18 clearly illustrates the limits of wisdom.

Discuss: Why is there much vexation in much wisdom, and why does he who increases knowledge also increase sorrow? *(Kind of like the saying, "Ignorance is bliss": as we grow wiser and become more aware, there are a lot of unpleasant things we learn about that can cause us worry and sadness.)*

The big idea of Ecclesiastes 1 is that life is *hebel*. That doesn't mean that everything in life is vain or meaningless, but it does mean it is hard to grasp, like smoke. It does not last, and it is confusing. In our next lesson, the Teacher will emphasize that life is *hebel* as he desperately searches to find significance… somewhere…anywhere!

Live Deeply: Guest Speakers

A major idea in this week's lesson is that life is *hebel:* like a breath on a cold day or a puff of smoke, it is something that doesn't last and is hard to grasp.

Sometimes it is hard for teenagers to understand this because they are young and feel like their whole lives are ahead of them. Furthermore, the daily grind of going to school seems long and monotonous, and perhaps even this Bible class period has seemed to take forever!

Life can also be hard for teenagers to understand, but the common assumption is that once they grow up, they will be able to figure things out. Those of us who are a little older know how mistaken that notion is!

When you talk to older adults and ask them to reflect on their lives, though, the response is consistent: it is amazing how quickly time passes, and we never understand all the things that we wish we did.

Invite two or three older Christians from your church to come and speak to your class. Have them reflect on the fleeting nature of life, aspects of life that have been hard for them to understand, and the trust in God that has brought them hope and meaning in life.

A DESPERATE SEARCH FOR MEANING
ECCLESIASTES 2

The Point

In this lesson, we will look at different ways in which people desperately search for meaning and significance in life, and how these pursuits are ultimately unfulfilling.

Dive In: How the World Finds Meaning

Divide your students into small groups and have them make lists of the sorts of things that people spend their lives chasing after (fame, fortune, popularity, cars, accomplishments, relationships, etc.). After a few minutes, compile the lists from the different groups and make a master list on a dry erase board. After discussing the different places where the Teacher searches for meaning in Ecclesiastes 2, bring your students' attention back to the list they made.

Most likely, the lists will be very, very similar. Truly the Teacher is correct in his assertion that there is nothing new under the sun! (Ecclesiastes 1.9-10).

Ecclesiastes 2.1-11

*I said in my heart, "Come now, I will test you with **pleasure**; enjoy yourself." But behold, this also was vanity. I said of **laughter**, "It is mad," and of pleasure, "What use is it?" I searched with my heart how to cheer my body with **wine**— my heart still guiding me with wisdom—and how to lay hold on **folly**, till I might see what was good for the children of man to do under heaven during the few days of their life. I made great **works**. I built **houses** and planted **vineyards** for myself. I made myself **gardens** and **parks**, and planted in them all kinds of **fruit trees**. I made myself **pools** from which to water the forest of growing trees. I bought **male and female slaves**, and had slaves who were born in my house. I had also great possessions of **herds and flocks**, more than any who had been before me in Jerusalem. I also gathered for myself **silver and gold** and the treasure of kings and provinces. I got **singers**, both men and women, and many **concubines**, the delight of the sons of man.*

*So I became **great** and surpassed all who were before me in Jerusalem. Also my **wisdom** remained with me. And whatever my eyes desired I did not keep from them. I kept my heart from no pleasure, for my heart found pleasure in all my **toil**, and this was my reward for all my toil. Then I considered all that my hands had done and the toil I had expended in doing it, and behold, all was vanity and a striving after wind, and there was nothing to be gained under the sun.*

A Desperate Search

Ecclesiastes 2 begins a well-known section of Ecclesiastes, as the Teacher pursues various pleasures in order to find meaning and significance in his life.

Discuss: As a class, generate a list of all the things the Teacher tries in order to find meaning and significance (see the bolded words in the text above). To switch things up a bit, you might have your students illustrate the different items on the board. How does this list compare with the list you made at the beginning of class of what people try today in order to find meaning and happiness in life?

Remember our *hebel* frame from last week's lesson: the point here is not that there is no meaning or significance in any of these pursuits (though some are certainly more important than others). The point is that they **do not last** and neither do they help us unlock the **mysterious** elements of life, so we should not build our lives on them. For example:

- Laughter is great, but a life built on laughter is a joke (pun intended)!
- Wisdom is good, but it has limitations (Ecclesiastes 1.18).
- Human relationships are an incredibly important part of our lives, but they are not the most foundational: if your life is built on a certain relationship, what happens when that relationship can no longer continue for some reason?

And so it goes with all that the Teacher tries. They are *hebel;* they are fleeting. We will not find lasting significance in them. Trying to find meaning in these vanities is like chasing after the wind or trying to grab hold of smoke: we will not succeed.

Ecclesiastes 2.12-17

So I turned to consider wisdom and madness and folly. For what can the man do who comes after the king? Only what has already been done. Then I saw that there is more gain in

> *wisdom than in folly, as there is more gain in light than in darkness. The wise person has his eyes in his head, but the fool walks in darkness. And yet I perceived that the same event happens to all of them. Then I said in my heart, "What happens to the fool will happen to me also. Why then have I been so very wise?" And I said in my heart that this also is vanity. For of the wise as of the fool there is no enduring remembrance, seeing that in the days to come all will have been long forgotten. How the wise dies just like the fool! So I hated life, because what is done under the sun was grievous to me, for all is vanity and a striving after wind.*

Now, the Teacher moves on to consider wisdom in more detail, and he does see that wisdom is better than the alternative, which is foolishness. It is preferable to be a wise man rather than a fool (this is the main point of Proverbs).

But even still, ultimately the same outcome happens to both the wise man and the foolish man: they both die! This might sound pretty pessimistic to us; if both the wise man and the foolish man die in the end, what difference does it make? Why not just be a fool? Again, this is *hebel*: some parts of life are hard to understand.

Still, we need to remember a couple of important truths. First, regardless of the certainty of death, the wise will generally live a more fulfilling life than the foolish and leave behind a better legacy (even if that legacy is only temporary). Also, as Christians we know that this life is not the end, but that how we live our lives *now* impacts our eternal destinies.[24]

---

[24] McMillion.

Ecclesiastes 2.18-23

I hated all my toil in which I toil under the sun, seeing that I must leave it to the man who will come after me, and who knows whether he will be wise or a fool? Yet he will be master of all for which I toiled and used my wisdom under the sun. This also is vanity. So I turned about and gave my heart up to despair over all the toil of my labors under the sun, because sometimes a person who has toiled with wisdom and knowledge and skill must leave everything to be enjoyed by someone who did not toil for it. This also is vanity and a great evil. What has a man from all the toil and striving of heart with which he toils beneath the sun? For all his days are full of sorrow, and his work is a vexation. Even in the night his heart does not rest. This also is vanity.

Here, the Teacher continues his pessimistic thought and focuses on the fleeting nature of our life's work. Ultimately, this is also not where we find meaning. After we are gone, our work has to be handed off to someone else; what if all we have worked years to build is destroyed in a heartbeat by the laziness or incompetence of someone else?

One of my best friends bought his first house, and for the few years that he lived there, spent a lot of time beautifying and landscaping outside. He dug up and removed ugly bushes, made flower beds, and planted fruit trees. In the springtime, beautiful flowers would bloom. It all took a lot of work, but he was proud of what he had accomplished.

Then the time came when it was necessary for him to sell his house and move elsewhere. A few months after the sale was finalized, he was near his old neighborhood and decided to drive by his old house. Imagine his shock and frustration when he saw that all of his flowers and flower beds, all of his hard work, had been dug up and destroyed! There was nothing to show for it! Toil is *hebel*! It does not last!

The Teacher here presents a lesson that a lot of Americans (myself included) need to hear: the danger of being a workaholic! Obsessing over our jobs makes our days "full of sorrow" and turns our work into a "vexation." That perhaps suggests the negative impact that being a workaholic can have on our health, but it can also destroy our families.

> ### Go Deeper: America's Great Addiction
>
> It is becoming increasingly clear that in the US, we are a nation of workaholics. Americans work longer days than any other industrialized nation, take less vacation, and retire later as well.[25] Consider some of these American statistics:[26]
>
> - 85.8% of men and 66.5% of women work over 40 hours per week.
> - From 1970 to 2006, the average number of hours of work people do per year has increased by 200.
> - 70% of kids in the US live in households where all adults are employed.
> - One in three American adults does not take his/her vacation days.
> - One in two workaholics' marriages ends with a divorce.
> - 60% of workaholics spend less than 20 minutes eating during lunch.
>
> This is clearly not a healthy trend, and it is one we would avoid if we paid attention to the teaching of Ecclesiastes!

---

[25] Dean Schabner, "Americans Work More Than Anyone," *ABC News.com*, May 1, 2014, http://abcnews.go.com/US/story?id=93364 (accessed November 29, 2014).

[26] These statistics can be found online at http://www.businessinsurance.org/workaholism/

Ecclesiastes 2.24-26

There is nothing better for a person than that he should eat and drink and find enjoyment in his toil. This also, I saw, is from the hand of God, for apart from him who can eat or who can have enjoyment? For to the one who pleases him God has given wisdom and knowledge and joy, but to the sinner he has given the business of gathering and collecting, only to give to one who pleases God. This also is vanity and a striving after wind.

Finally, the chapter ends with some more optimistic thinking. Based on the conclusions of 2.24-26, the solution to the *hebel* of work is not to quit your job or to despair. Instead, we should enjoy our work, our food, and our drink. These are concrete blessings that God has given us, and we should accept them with gratitude now. We shouldn't obsess over the future, our significance, our legacy, or anything else; we should appreciate the simple blessings of life that God has given us.[27]

---

[27] Bland, 322, "There is no compulsive or obsessive attitude about enjoyment at this point. Rather than pursuing enjoyment, Qoheleth accepts it as a gift."

Discuss: How do you feel about the Teacher's evaluation of work?

In Ecclesiastes 2, we see the great lengths to which the Teacher went in search of meaning: wealth, pleasure, accomplishments, relationships, wisdom, and work. But he concluded that all of it was *hebel*. None of it lasts, and if we try to find lasting significance in any of these pursuits it will be like trying to chase after the wind: absolutely futile.

> ### Live Deeply: Finding Balance in our Work
>
> We've already discussed workaholism and how it is not good or healthy. Workaholism is a major problem with adults, but, sometimes, the problem for teenagers is just the opposite: laziness.
>
> Lead a discussion with your class focusing on their school studies as being their "job". Discuss the need for **balance** in their approach to their studies, avoiding obsessive workaholism on one hand, and neglectful laziness on the other. Consider Ecclesiastes 2.18-23, Colossians 3.17, and Colossians 3.23 in your discussion.

THE SEASONS OF LIFE
ECCLESIASTES 3

The Point

This lesson will emphasize that there are different "seasons" of life and that it is important for us to appreciate where we are in life and make the most of it.

Dive In: *Dead Poets' Society*

To help introduce Ecclesiastes 3 to your students, show a short clip (about three minutes long) from the movie *Dead Poets Society*.[28]

In this scene, Mr. Keating, the character played by Robin Williams, emphasizes to his students that life passes quickly and, therefore, it is important that we make the most of the time we have.

---

[28] *Dead Poets Society,* directed by Peter Weir, Touchstone Pictures, 1989, https://www.youtube.com/watch?v=vi0Lbjs5ECI.

"Carpe Diem!" he encourages his students. "Seize the day, boys! Make your lives extraordinary!"

As we shall see, this is a message that the Teacher of Ecclesiastes would want his students to understand as well.

Ecclesiastes 3.1-8

For everything there is a season, and a time for every matter under heaven:

> *a time to be born, and a time to die;*
> *a time to plant, and a time to pluck up what is planted;*
> *a time to kill, and a time to heal;*
> *a time to break down, and a time to build up;*
> *a time to weep, and a time to laugh;*
> *a time to mourn, and a time to dance;*
> *a time to cast away stones, and a time to gather stones together;*
> *a time to embrace, and a time to refrain from embracing;*
> *a time to seek, and a time to lose;*
> *a time to keep, and a time to cast away;*
> *a time to tear, and a time to sew;*
> *a time to keep silence, and a time to speak;*
> *a time to love, and a time to hate;*
> *a time for war, and a time for peace.*

A Time for Everything

Here we have one of the most famous sections in all of Ecclesiastes, and it may be familiar to some of your students.[29]

---

[29] These verses actually serve as the inspiration for a once-famous song from The Byrds, which you may want to play for your students: https://www.youtube.com/watch?v=W4ga_M5Zdn4&safe=active

DISCUSS: What is the point of this poem?

This poem does not mean that God determines every little detail of life, but it does suggest that "God determines the broad order of human events and experiences."[30]

There is a cycle to our lives, and everything (even circumstances or events that we may perceive to be "bad") has its proper place within that cycle. It is when things happen *outside* of their proper place in the cycle that it seems that life has gone horribly wrong. For example, a person is born and grows up, and we expect that person to die at some point. But we expect it to be when the person is old; it's when someone dies when they are still young that we feel something is out of place.

This cycle also suggests a certain balance to life—when you look at the pairings in the poem we just read, it is not healthy to have one without the other:

- It doesn't work to plant all the time; you have to plant at the right time of year, give the soil time to replenish nutrients, etc.
- In life, there are times when we should be happy, and there are other times when it's necessary to be sad. In our society, we like to avoid sadness and so we are often nervous about attending funerals. Even at funerals we sometimes try to turn them into happy events, but when someone we care about has died, it is absolutely appropriate that we mourn and weep, and it is healthy to do so.
- There are times when we really need to keep our mouths shut, and there are other times when we need to speak out. Think of Job's friends: they would have comforted Job a lot more if they would have just kept their mouths shut. On the other hand, think of a situation at school when someone is being bullied or made fun of. In those situations, we need to

---
[30] Bland, 326.

- speak out and do what we can to stand up for the person being oppressed.
- As horrible as we tend to think war is, there's a time when that is appropriate as well. World War II was a horribly tragic event, but it was necessary to put a stop to the evil that was being perpetrated by Adolf Hitler and Nazi Germany. Of course, that doesn't mean that we should constantly be at war; there is a time for peace as well!

Ecclesiastes 3.9-15

What gain has the worker from his toil? I have seen the business that God has given to the children of man to be busy with. He has made everything beautiful in its time. Also, He has put eternity into man's heart, yet so that he cannot find out what God has done from the beginning to the end. I perceived that there is nothing better for them than to be joyful and to do good as long as they live; also that everyone should eat and drink and take pleasure in all his toil–this is God's gift to man.

I perceived that whatever God does endures forever; nothing can be added to it, nor anything taken from it. God has done it, so that people fear before Him. That which is, already has been; that which is to be, already has been; and God seeks what has been driven away.

Ecclesiastes 3.11 is important: *"He has made everything beautiful in its time."*

DISCUSS:

- Does all we discussed in 3.1-8 seem beautiful?
- Why do you think God allows "bad" things like death and war to occur?

- **What does it mean for everything to be "beautiful" in its time?**

These verses are a helpful reminder that our perceptions of whether or not something is good or bad are limited. Ever since the Garden of Eden, humans have been seeking to define good and bad on our own terms, but it is God who tells us what is good. In this context, "beautiful" means that which is suitable for the occasion—God has made everything fitting or appropriate for its time.[31]

There are many experiences that we will have in life, but those things will occur in their own time, and *right now* might not be the right time for some of those experiences. Humans have this tendency—and I think it is especially true for teenagers—to always be looking ahead and wishing that we were in a different season of life.

I once came across this poem and thought it offered a good perspective:

I Was Dying

First I was dying to finish high school and start college.
And then I was dying to finish college and start working.
And then I was dying to marry and have children.
And then I was dying for my children to grow old
enough for school so I could return to work.
And then I was dying to retire.
And now, I am dying…and suddenly I realize I forgot to live.

(Anonymous)

---

[31] Bland, 327.

If God has made everything beautiful in its time, that means that we should be careful about wishing away our lives. Instead, we should take advantage of what we have been given and make the most of it in each moment. Remember the scene from *Dead Poets Society* that we watched earlier: "Carpe Diem! Seize the day! Make your lives extraordinary!"

In some ways, this is like the YOLO! saying that was popular several years ago, except the idea is not, "You only live once, so let's do crazy and reckless things!" Rather, the idea is, "You only live once, so let's take advantage of the time God has given us and make the most of it!"[32] We should make the most of the season we are in, and eat, drink, and take pleasure in our work—these are gifts from God!

Ecclesiastes 3.11 is also a famous verse: *"[God] has put eternity into man's heart, yet so that he cannot find out what God has done from the beginning to the end."*

DISCUSS: What do you think this means?

As Christians, whenever we think of "eternity", we tend to immediately think of eternity with God, but I am not sure that this is what the Teacher has in mind. More likely, I think it refers to the fact that as humans, we have some concept of eternity. We realize how small and insignificant we are, that the world was here long before we were born, and that it will likely continue long after we are gone. It is God who is eternal, who directs eternity, and it is only through His revelation that we can have some understanding of it. Left to our own wisdom and attempts to figure life out, life is *hebel*; it is impenetrable and mysterious.

---

[32] Brown, 149.

Ecclesiastes 3.16-22

Moreover, I saw under the sun that in the place of justice, even there was wickedness, and in the place of righteousness, even there was wickedness. I said in my heart, God will judge the righteous and the wicked, for there is a time for every matter and for every work. I said in my heart with regard to the children of man that God is testing them that they may see that they themselves are but beasts. For what happens to the children of man and what happens to the beasts is the same; as one dies, so dies the other. They all have the same breath, and man has no advantage over the beasts, for all is vanity. All go to one place. All are from the dust, and to dust all return. Who knows whether the spirit of man goes upward and the spirit of the beast goes down into the earth? So I saw that there is nothing better than that a man should rejoice in his work, for that is his lot. Who can bring him to see what will be after him?

To end the chapter, the Teacher talks about judgment and death. Speaking of judgment, he looks at the world around him and sees wickedness and injustice, but he trusts that God is just and will ultimately bring judgment upon evil in His own time.

Regarding death, the Teacher basically says that we are like animals in the sense that, once breath leaves our bodies, we are dead. Focusing on death makes sense after a discussion of the cycle of life, and also fits with the repeated emphasis of *hebel*: life is fleeting and hard to comprehend. There *is* a time to die. That is true for us just like it is for animals. For all of our intelligence and our capabilities, that fact still unites us: we will die.[33]

Live Deeply: Making the Most of our Time

Have your students make a list of things that they wish they were old enough to do. They will likely mention things like driving, going to college, getting married, and having children. Affirm the value of these things, but also remind them that God takes care of us and has arranged that different events happen at different times in our lives.

Ecclesiastes offers us the wise perspective that we should focus on enjoying and making the most of the season of life we are currently in rather than always wishing for the next thing.

---

[33] This does not mean that there is no difference between us and animals, but it does suggest an underlying similarity that we share as God's creatures: God gives us the breath of life, and when it is gone, we die.

BARRIERS TO JOY
ECCLESIASTES 4

The Point

This lesson will look at different attitudes and circumstances in life that will rob us of joy if we are not careful.

Dive In: The Strength of Teamwork

Ecclesiastes 4.9-12 discusses the value of having companions and the strength that comes from combining our energies and abilities. We are stronger together than we are alone!

To illustrate this, give each of your students a marker and a strip of cloth (different colors would be nice). Have them write their names at the very end of their cloth. Then have them test the strength of their cloth by pulling on it, trying to loop it under a chair and lift it up, etc. After a few minutes, put the students in groups of three and have them braid their strips of cloth together. When they've finished, test the strength of their combined cloth as before. After a few more minutes, have these groups combine with other groups and make a larger braid out of the three group braids. Again, test the strength of this braid.

Then, read Ecclesiastes 4.12 and ask the following questions:
- How does the strength of your group braid compare to the strength of your individual cloth?
- How is the braid similar to people working together?
- In what ways are we stronger together than apart?
- How do the different colors of our combined braid illustrate our group?

After finishing the discussion and accompanying lesson, display the group braid in your youth room as a reminder of the value of unity and teamwork within your youth group.[34]

Ecclesiastes 4.1-16

Again I saw all the oppressions that are done under the sun. And behold, the tears of the oppressed, and they had no one to comfort them! On the side of their oppressors there was power, and there was no one to comfort them. And I thought the dead who are already dead more fortunate than the living who are still alive. But better than both is he who has not yet been and has not seen the evil deeds that are done under the sun.

Then I saw that all toil and all skill in work come from a man's envy of his neighbor. This also is vanity and a striving after wind.

The fool folds his hands and eats his own flesh.

Better is a handful of quietness than two hands full of toil and a striving after wind.

Again, I saw vanity under the sun: one person who has no other, either son or brother, yet there is no end to all his toil,

---

[34] Debbie Gowensmith, ed., *PointMaker: Object Lessons for Youth Ministry* (Loveland, CO: Group, 2000), 24-25.

and his eyes are never satisfied with riches, so that he never asks, "For whom am I toiling and depriving myself of pleasure?" This also is vanity and an unhappy business.

Two are better than one, because they have a good reward for their toil. For if they fall, one will lift up his fellow. But woe to him who is alone when he falls and has not another to lift him up! Again, if two lie together, they keep warm, but how can one keep warm alone? And though a man might prevail against one who is alone, two will withstand him—a threefold cord is not quickly broken.

Better was a poor and wise youth than an old and foolish king who no longer knew how to take advice. For he went from prison to the throne, though in his own kingdom he had been born poor. I saw all the living who move about under the sun, along with that youth who was to stand in the king's place. There was no end of all the people, all of whom he led. Yet those who come later will not rejoice in him. Surely this also is vanity and a striving after wind.

Things that Keep us from Joy

When we looked at Ecclesiastes 3, we discussed the cycles of life. We emphasized that there are appropriate times for the highs and lows of life, and how it is important to intentionally try to make the most of our current situation in life instead of constantly wishing our lives away and looking for what comes next.

In Ecclesiastes 3, the Teacher seemed fairly optimistic as he advised that we seek to make the most of our time in life and enjoy it, but Ecclesiastes 4 takes a more negative turn, as he discusses some barriers that limit our joy: **oppression** (4.1-3), envy (4.4-6), **loneliness** (4.7-12), and the **fleeting nature of power** (4.13-16).[35]

OPPRESSION (4.1-3)

To start, the Teacher makes some observations about the harshness of life, and specifically in regards to **oppression.**

Perhaps we will understand the Teacher's perspective better if we realize that the ancient world was very different from the society in which we live in the United States. There was virtually no middle class; instead, there were only a few who were very rich and then a lot of extremely poor people who worked long hours for very little return. The poor had little legal protection to prevent them from being taken advantage of or cheated by the wealthy who had power over them.[36]

EGYPTIAN PEASANT LABORERS

This was a very common feature of the ancient world, and it was true of Israel as well. In fact, one of the major themes of the Old Testament prophets is God's displeasure with the wealthy for victimizing and taking advantage of the poor. Sadly, this same situation occurs in many places today as well.

In this setting, the Teacher looks around at the widespread oppression in his world and really doesn't see much hope:

---

[35] Cook, 98.

[36] McMillion.

what can be done? He says it would be better to be dead than to continue to suffer such oppression. Better than that would be to never be born and never witness it in the first place![37]

DISCUSS:

- We've already mentioned that our society is significantly different from ancient societies; is injustice and oppression still something that happens in our society?
- What should be our response to problems like these when we witness them?

It is important to notice that at the end of this section, the Teacher includes the "under the sun" tagline that refers to all of human life and experience.[38] The sad reality is that, apart from the influence of God and the ethical values that He wants people to embrace, people will often choose to victimize one another. As Christians, we should be very deliberate about confronting the evil and oppression that goes on "under the sun" with Kingdom values.

ENVY (4.4-6)

The Teacher moves on to address the topic of **envy.** Ecclesiastes 4.4 perhaps serves as a theme verse for this small section, and has an interesting suggestion: how often is our hard work and achievement based on the fact that we envy what other people have and want to outdo them? Do we work hard because we care about our jobs or the companies we work for, or do we work hard so we can have a better title than

---

[37] The Teacher's statement here should be taken as hyperbole rather than his absolute perspective, because later, in Ecclesiastes 9.4-5, he will emphasize that life is preferable to death: "a living dog is better than a dead lion." These seeming contradictions represent the emotional exasperation that the Teacher experiences as he considers the *hebel* of the world around him.

[38] Bland, 311.

someone else or so that we can afford to buy a nicer car than our neighbors? The Teacher points out that this is useless: it is like striving after the wind, and he again refers to it as vanity—it lacks in real significance and will not last.

Ecclesiastes 4.5-6 sound like proverbs (remember that Ecclesiastes is Wisdom Literature), which seem a little confusing at first glance.

DISCUSS: Any ideas on what these mean?

It seems like this is a comparison between the really ambitious and the lazy: while some people obsessively work so they can have what others have, other people choose instead to be lazy and do nothing. Ecclesiastes 4.6 suggests that neither of these extreme positions are the answer. Instead, it is better to be pleased with what you have than to obsessively strive for what you don't have.

LONELINESS (4.7-12)

Next, we have some very important comments about **loneliness** and the importance of companionship. The Teacher says it is good to have people in your life whom you care about and with whom you can share the fruits of your labors. In Ecclesiastes 2 we talked about the dangers of being a workaholic; at the same time, the knowledge that we work to provide for people we care about helps to motivate us to work hard. Working for the benefit of someone else helps our work to be more meaningful.[39]

There are also words here about the value of companionship in general: companionship is good. There's a Swedish Proverb that says, "Shared joy is a double joy; shared sorrow is half a sorrow." When we are celebrating a birthday or some other significant event, the fun increases if we are surrounded by

---
[39] Bland, 335.

> **Shared JOY is a DOUBLE JOY;**
> **Shared SORROW is HALF a SORROW.**

friends. If we are going through a difficult time, being around our friends helps to bring us comfort. Remember our group activity at the start of the lesson: in many ways, we are stronger together than we are on our own.

FLEETING NATURE OF POWER (4.13-16)

Finally, Ecclesiastes 4 ends with a discussion of the **fleeting nature of power**. There are some pretty negative words about the king here, and if you think back to our opening lesson, sections like this are one of the reasons that many people doubt that King Solomon wrote Ecclesiastes: would someone who was a king be so negative about kings?[40]

The basic idea here seems to be that being a king isn't so great if you are a foolish king. Furthermore, regardless of what a king does or how many people he leads, his reign is *hebel;* it is fleeting and will come to an end, and those after him will forget all about him.

---

[40] See pages 12-15 for a fuller discussion on the authorship of Ecclesiastes.

Live Deeply: Making a Difference Together

To emphasize again the strength that comes from combining our abilities and working together, organize a day of service projects at your church where your teenagers can partner with adult Christians to do good works for people in your community (mowing lawns, raking leaves, visiting shut-ins, washing cars, donating clothes, etc.).

Afterwards, have a discussion with your class reflecting on how much more they were able to accomplish together than any of them would have been able to do on their own.

ENJOYING GOD'S GIFTS
ECCLESIASTES 5

The Point

According to Ecclesiastes, a crucial element of enjoying life is viewing everything we have as gifts from God, and appreciating them *as* gifts.

Dive In: Your Favorite Gifts

To introduce this lesson, get feedback from your students on the following questions:

1. What is one of your favorite gifts (birthday, Christmas, etc.) that you have ever received? What is it about this gift that makes it one of your favorites?
2. What are some examples of different kinds of gifts that God gives to people?
3. What are some specific gifts that God has given to you?

When we realize that all that we have comes from God, it radically changes our perspective on life.

Ecclesiastes 5.1-7

Guard your steps when you go to the house of God. To draw near to listen is better than to offer the sacrifice of fools, for they do not know that they are doing evil. Be not rash with your mouth, nor let your heart be hasty to utter a word before God, for God is in heaven and you are on earth. Therefore let your words be few. For a dream comes with much business, and a fool's voice with many words.

When you vow a vow to God, do not delay paying it, for He has no pleasure in fools. Pay what you vow. It is better that you should not vow than that you should vow and not pay. Let not your mouth lead you into sin, and do not say before the messenger that it was a mistake. Why should God be angry at your voice and destroy the work of your hands? For when dreams increase and words grow many, there is vanity; but God is the One you must fear.

Being Wise before God

So far, the Teacher has made many observations about life but hasn't spent much time speaking directly about our relationship with God. That changes in the first section of Ecclesiastes 5.

Discuss: What is the "house of God" mentioned here? Do we have a "house of God" today? *(Make sure to distinguish between the Temple, our church buildings, and our bodies.)*

The Teacher talks about being careful and reverent in the way we approach God, and this is not an uncommon idea in Scripture. In fact, one of the themes that we see repeated throughout the Old Testament prophets is how much it frustrates God when His people come to worship Him and go through the motions of religious devotion, but then their daily lives don't match that devotion. We should always strive to live in such a way that the person we look like on Sunday is the same person we resemble the rest of the week. Otherwise, our worship is empty and without meaning.

The Teacher also gives a good deal of advice regarding the need to be careful with our words. A significant aspect of being wise is knowing when to talk and when to keep our mouths shut; some of us who are naturally quiet need wisdom to know when to speak up *more*, while others of us who are naturally talkative need wisdom to know when to keep quiet.

DISCUSS: "God is in heaven and you are on earth." What is the point of saying this?

The Teacher is not saying that God is so distant that we cannot know or understand Him. After all, God *wants* us to know and understand Him; that is what the Word becoming flesh and living among us was all about—Jesus came to show us the Father (John 1.14).

Still, this verse is a recognition that God is distinct from us. He is sovereign and sits upon the throne of the universe. We do not control God by our worship. We cannot manipulate God into doing what we want with good church attendance!

Ecclesiastes 5.4-5 discusses how we need to be wise in making vows to God. If you promise something to God, pay what you vow; it would be better to make no promise at all than to promise and then not follow through. For example, we need to be really careful about saying "I'll pray for you" to people unless we really are going to follow through on that promise and pray for that person. "I'll pray for you" is not a flippant response we give to someone who is struggling in order to make them feel better; it is a promise that we will intercede on their behalf with the Creator of the universe. We should be careful about *all* the promises we make, but especially the promises we make concerning God and spiritual matters.

> ## Go Deeper: Jephthah's Foolish Vow
>
> Judges 11 tells the story of Jephthah, a mighty warrior who God used to deliver the Israelites from the Ammonites.
>
> Before going into battle, Jephthah made a vow to God saying that if the Lord would give him victory, he would sacrifice as a burnt offering whatever came out of the doors of his house to meet him upon his return (Judges 11.30-31).
>
> Jephthah achieved a great military victory and delivered Israel from the Ammonites, but when he returned home, his only child, a daughter, came out of his house to cheer his victory. Remembering the rash vow he had made, Jephthah tore his robes and lamented.
>
> Scholars disagree about whether or not Jephthah actually offered his daughter as a burnt offering, or whether he "offered" her to the Lord by dedicating her to His service for the rest of her life.[41] Either way, Jephthah made a foolish promise to God without first considering the possible consequences, and his daughter's life was forever changed as a result.
>
> In Ecclesiastes, the Teacher warns us against such foolishness.

---

[41] For a summary of the different viewpoints, see Wayne Jackson, "What About Jephthah's Vow?," *Christian Courier*, https://www.christiancourier.com/articles/1081-what-about-jephthahs-vow (accessed July 14, 2021).

DISCUSS: What does it mean to fear God? (5.7)

The idea of fearing God is important in Ecclesiastes. This does *not* mean that we should live our lives in terror of God. Some people have a view of God that He is always on the lookout to see when we mess up so He can zap us. When I was little, this idea is always what I thought of when I heard the song, "There's an All-Seeing Eye Watching You." To be sure, God *does* see all things and He *is* watching us, but God is not the Cosmic Creeper. God is powerful and He punishes evil, but those who seek to obey Him have no reason to live in terror of Him.

The idea of fearing God occurs several times in the Bible outside of Ecclesiastes. One of those times is in Exodus 18 where Jethro, the father-in-law of Moses, gives him some advice. Whenever the people had a dispute, they brought it before Moses so he could make a judgment on what to do. Jethro realized that this would eventually wear Moses out because it was too much for one person to do, and he suggests that Moses get some men to help him settle these matters. In Exodus 18.21, he says, *"Moreover, look for able men from all the people,* **men who fear God,** *who are trustworthy and hate a bribe, and place such men over the people as chiefs of thousands, of hundreds, of fifties, and of tens."*

JETHRO AND MOSES

In this context, fearing God has to do with being an honest and upright person. In other words, we "fear God" by respecting His ethical and moral demands for our lives.

Ecclesiastes 5.8-17

If you see in a province the oppression of the poor and the violation of justice and righteousness, do not be amazed at the matter, for the high official is watched by a higher, and there are yet higher ones over them. But this is gain for a land in every way: a king committed to cultivated fields.

He who loves money will not be satisfied with money, nor he who loves wealth with his income; this also is vanity. When goods increase, they increase who eat them, and what advantage has their owner but to see them with his eyes? Sweet is the sleep of a laborer, whether he eats little or much, but the full stomach of the rich will not let him sleep.

There is a grievous evil that I have seen under the sun: riches were kept by their owner to his hurt, and those riches were lost in a bad venture. And he is father of a son, but he has nothing in his hand. As he came from his mother's womb he shall go again, naked as he came, and shall take nothing for his toil that he may carry away in his hand. This also is a grievous evil: just as he came, so shall he go, and what gain is there to him who toils for the wind? Moreover, all his days he eats in darkness in much vexation and sickness and anger.

In an echo of Ecclesiastes 4, this next section discusses economic injustice and oppression, which the Teacher asserts is widespread and something that we should not be surprised by. Most likely, the point here is not that there is a chain of command where higher officials keep lower officials in check, but instead the Teacher is describing a "dishonest bureaucracy, a whole network of corruption" where public officials are mainly interested in their own gain.[42]

In contrast to this, "a king committed to cultivated fields" (5.9)—a leader who will take responsibility for the economic wellbeing of his people and seek justice—is of great benefit to society.

The main topic in this section, though, is money, and the Teacher has some important insights regarding it. The harshest feedback I have ever received when preaching came after I delivered a sermon about money. People don't like it when you meddle with how they use money, but here is the problem with that: the Bible talks about money all the time! Jesus spoke about money frequently, and we find teachings on it throughout Scripture (including here in Ecclesiastes). If we want to be biblical, we will talk about money a lot!

If you remember from earlier chapters, the Teacher was incredibly wealthy, knew all about what money could buy, and he said it was *hebel*. It doesn't last, it doesn't provide answers to life's mysterious questions, and it doesn't provide real significance. Here he goes on to list some of the traps that money can lead us into.

DISCUSS: As a class, list the problems that money can bring which the Teacher mentions in Ecclesiastes 5.10-15.[43]

- Addiction/dissatisfaction (5.10)
- Attracts the greedy (5.11)
- Becomes a status symbol/trophy (5.11)
- Promotes worry (5.12)

---

[42] Bland, 341.

[43] This helpful list comes from Chad Landman, *Wisdom for Life: 6 Weeks in Ecclesiastes* (Hashtag Media, 2013), 18.

- Causes lack of sleep (5.12)
- Leads to hoarding/stockpiling (5.13)
- It is easily lost (5.14)
- Cannot follow us after death (5.15-17)

DISCUSS: Is money inherently bad? Before answering, read Matthew 19.16-26 and 1 Timothy 6.9-10 as a class.

Money is *not* inherently bad, but Scripture has much to say about wealth that should make us very careful in how we view it. Money can very easily become bad for us. We need to look at our money and, indeed, all of our material possessions, as being on loan from God. All that we have belongs to God, and He gives us our possessions so that we can use them for His glory. Therefore, we should take care of our money and be good stewards of it, but we should always remember that it isn't really ours. Keeping that in mind will help us not to get too attached to it, and also to look for ways we can use it to help others and glorify God.

Ecclesiastes 5.18-20

Behold, what I have seen to be good and fitting is to eat and drink and find enjoyment in all the toil with which one toils under the sun the few days of his life that God has given him, for this is his lot. Everyone also to whom God has given wealth and possessions and power to enjoy them, and to accept his lot and rejoice in his toil—this is the gift of God. For he will not much remember the days of his life because God keeps him occupied with joy in his heart.

Ecclesiastes 5 ends with another summary statement emphasizing the importance of enjoying the blessings that God has given us (cf. 2.24-26). Work is good; we were created to be workers. When God created Adam, He placed him in the garden and told him to tend it. From the beginning, humans were intended to be workers. There are many people who are disabled and cannot work, and many more who need jobs to provide for their families but cannot find them; these are unfortunate situations. If you are able to work and have a job, that is a blessing. If you enjoy your work and enjoy the people you work with, that is an even greater blessing.

In Ecclesiastes, the Teacher is clear that there is much about life that is *hebel* and hard to figure out (like widespread oppression, the way we die just like animals do, or the way we leave behind everything when we die), but he does know that work, food, and family are blessings from the Lord and should be enjoyed as such.[44] When we think of these things as **gifts** rather than **achievements**, it really changes our perspective. These are blessings God bestows on us to enjoy, not objectives for us to obsessively strive after. There is a lot of joy to be found in living a simple life: "constructive work, sufficient food, and fellowship" are what we really need.[45] Enjoying these things as gifts from God is one of the Teacher's most important lessons.

> ### Live Deeply: Blessings Journals
> For a week, have your students keep a journal to record the blessings God has given them and the ways in which they are seeking to enjoy these gifts.

---

[44] McMillion.

[45] Brown, 136.

THE VALUE OF CONTENTMENT
ECCLESIASTES 6

The Point

When we fail to appreciate the blessings of life, we become discontented and miserable.

Dive In: An Olympic Disappointment

Have you ever struggled to be content with what you have accomplished or with what you have?

McKayla Maroney, a gymnast on the 2012 U.S. Olympic Team, became famous when she very publicly displayed her disappointment after receiving a silver medal in the vault

McKAYLA MARONEY
2012 OLYMPIC VAULT
SILVER MEDALIST

competition. Maroney was the overwhelming favorite to win the event, but finished second after falling during her routine. Most people in the world would be thrilled to win a silver medal at the Olympics, but Maroney disappointment was so great that she could not be content.

> ## Ecclesiastes 6.1-9
>
> *There is an evil that I have seen under the sun, and it lies heavy on mankind: a man to whom God gives wealth, possessions, and honor, so that he lacks nothing of all that he desires, yet God does not give him power to enjoy them, but a stranger enjoys them. This is vanity; it is a grievous evil. If a man fathers a hundred children and lives many years, so that the days of his years are many, but his soul is not satisfied with life's good things, and he also has no burial, I say that a stillborn child is better off than he. For it comes in vanity and goes in darkness, and in darkness its name is covered. Moreover, it has not seen the sun or known anything, yet it finds rest rather than he. Even though he should live a thousand years twice over, yet enjoy no good—do not all go to the one place?*
>
> *All the toil of man is for his mouth, yet his appetite is not satisfied. For what advantage has the wise man over the fool? And what does the poor man have who knows how to conduct himself before the living? Better is the sight of the eyes than the wandering of the appetite: this also is vanity and a striving after wind.*

Appreciating God's Blessings

Ecclesiastes 5 ended with the Teacher talking about how important it is that we recognize our blessings from God, and how we need to enjoy and appreciate them. In Ecclesiastes 6, the opposite situation is discussed: it is truly unfortunate when we are unable to enjoy the blessings God has given to us or when we are never satisfied with what we have.

The Teacher says that for those who are not satisfied with the blessings of life, even if they were to have a hundred children or live for two thousand years, it would be better if they had never been born! This is, of course, hyperbole, but the point is that if you aren't content, it doesn't matter what you have; you will always be miserable because you will always want more.[46]

This may sound pessimistic, but life doesn't *have* to be this way: eyes that see and recognize the blessings of God are better than a wandering appetite that can never be satisfied (6.9)!

Ecclesiastes 6.10-12

Whatever has come to be has already been named, and it is known what man is, and that he is not able to dispute with one stronger than he. The more words, the more vanity, and what is the advantage to man? For who knows what is good for man while he lives the few days of his vain life, which he passes like a shadow? For who can tell man what will be after him under the sun?

Ecclesiastes 6.10 says, *"Whatever has come to be has already been named, and it is known what man is, and that he is not able to dispute with one stronger than he."* This is somewhat of a confusing verse, but it seems to be a reminder of the limited control we have over our lives.

Sometimes when children are little, their parents tell them that

---

[46] Bland, 347, "The insatiable desire of humans that drives them to acquire more is a miserable sickness."

they can accomplish anything in life they want to (perhaps your parents told you this as well). Unfortunately, it just isn't true! Certainly, God has given us amazing abilities and opportunities, and when we combine those talents and opportunities with hard work and the support of friends and family, we can achieve much. But there are limits to what we can do, and there are some circumstances over which we simply don't have much control. Not every child can grow up to be the President of the United States or to be a professional baseball player. Some children don't get to grow up *at all*; their lives are snatched away by cancer, or a car accident, or some other terrible tragedy that prevents them from even *trying* to accomplish their goals.

The point is that in the grand scheme of things, we have very little control over our lives, and this is another reason we should seek contentment. Since we are limited in what we can do to truly change our lives, we should find contentment in the blessings God has given us.

In 6.12, the Teacher asks, *"Who knows what is good for man while he lives the few days of his vain life, which he passes like a shadow?"* This verse reminds us of the dual meaning of *hebel*: life is both fleeting ("few days", "shadow") and hard to understand ("who knows?").

DISCUSS: What are some different reasons that people are not able to enjoy their blessings or are not satisfied with what they have? *(We worry about what will happen when we are gone; addictive behavior/never getting enough; searching for meaning through possessions; misunderstanding contentment; envying others.)*

Contentment is less about *what* you have and more about your attitude of thankfulness *toward* what you have. A New Testament passage that has much to say on this topic is

Philippians 4.10-13: *"I rejoiced in the Lord greatly that now at length you have revived your concern for me. You were indeed concerned for me, but you had no opportunity. Not that I am speaking of being in need, for I have learned in whatever situation I am to be content. I know how to be brought low, and I know how to abound. In any and every circumstance, I have learned the secret of facing plenty and hunger, abundance and need. I can do all things through Him who strengthens me."*

PAUL
CONTENT IN ALL CIRCUMSTANCES

Paul says that he has learned to be content in whatever situation he finds himself. That confirms that contentment is an *internal* quality rather than an *external* one; it does not depend on the circumstances around us. Paul had a lot of difficulties in his life—he was beaten, imprisoned, scourged, left for dead, shipwrecked, etc.—but he was nevertheless able to find contentment.

This also helps us to better understand what Paul means when he famously says, "I can do all things through Christ who gives me strength." This verse is frequently taken out of context and abused, but Paul isn't talking here about passing an algebra test or winning a basketball game. Instead, what he means is that Jesus Christ empowers him to find contentment in all situations.

DISCUSS: Why is contentment so difficult for us? What can we do to be more at peace with our lives and to truly be content? *(Remember that our blessings are a gift from God; realize that there are different seasons in life; it is not our job to try and measure up to the standards of the world.)*

God bestows blessings on all people. Those who learn to look at what they have *as* blessings from God and appreciate those blessings will live happier, more fulfilled lives than those who can never be content.

> ### Live Deeply: Blessings Ledgers
>
> *Note: If students made Blessings Journals over the past week, those will be helpful in completing this exercise.*
>
> A lot of times, we struggle with contentment because we focus on the things we *don't* have rather than thinking about all the blessings that God has heaped upon us.
>
> Give your students a piece of paper and have them draw a line down the center so there are two big columns. This will function as their Blessings Ledger. Have them label one column "Needs" and the other "Blessings". Under the "Needs" column, have them make a list of the things in life that they *truly need* but do not have. Under the "Blessings" column, have them list all of the blessings God has given them (or at least, as many as they can think of). Make sure to allow your students several minutes to accomplish this, as it will take some time for them to come up with full lists.
>
> Then, have people volunteer to share items from each list. Some students will likely have some questionable "Needs", so make sure to discuss those when they come up. Ultimately, the results will be the same: there might be things we *want* that we don't have, but usually there is not much we *need* that we don't have. And even then, those needs are far outweighed by God's blessings. Taking stock of those blessings and enjoying them is a major part of being content.

GOD IS IN CONTROL
ECCLESIASTES 7

The Point

God's perspective is different than ours; even when life seems chaotic and out of control, God is still sovereign.

Dive In: Seeing the Whole Picture

Print off copies of the paragraph below for your students to read or write it out on the dry erase board for them. It might be surprising to them how easily they can read it:

> *Aoccdrnig to rscheearch at an Elingsh uinervtisy, it deosn't mttaer in waht oredr the ltteers in a wrod are, the olny iprmoetnt tihng is taht the frist and lsat ltteer is at the rghit pclae. The rset can be a toatl mses and you can sitll raed it wouthit a porbelm. Tihs is bcuseae we do not raed ervey lteter by istlef but the wrod as a wlohe.*

We might be pretty good at seeing words as a whole, but we struggle to see our lives that way. Instead, we get so caught up looking at the individual "letters"—whatever we may be experiencing in the moment—that we sometimes lose sight of the big picture. God is not like that, though. God does not *cause* all things, but He is in *control* of all things. He also has infinite knowledge of the past, present, and future, and that gives Him a much better perspective on the world than we have.

When bad things happen to us, it may seem that God is not in control. But when we look at the whole "word" of history rather than the individual "letters", we know that He is sovereign.

Ecclesiastes 7.1-8

A good name is better than precious ointment, and the day of death than the day of birth.

It is better to go to the house of mourning than to go to the house of feasting, for this is the end of all mankind, and the living will lay it to heart.

Sorrow is better than laughter, for by sadness of face the heart is made glad.

The heart of the wise is in the house of mourning, but the heart of fools is in the house of mirth.

It is better for a man to hear the rebuke of the wise than to hear the song of fools.

For as the crackling of thorns under a pot, so is the laughter of the fools; this also is vanity.

Surely oppression drives the wise into madness, and a bribe corrupts the heart.

Better is the end of a thing than its beginning, and the patient in spirit is better than the proud in spirit.

The Perspective at the End

Ecclesiastes 7 is a challenging chapter, so we will need to study it carefully. It begins with a series of proverbs where the

Teacher outlines several things that are "good" or "better". This seems a little confusing at first, considering that he has just asked in 6.12, *"For who knows what is good for man while he lives the few days of his vain life, which he passes like a shadow?"* Really, though, this is in accordance with what we repeatedly see in Ecclesiastes: although the Teacher at times seems to throw up his hands in despair at the elements of life that are uncertain or incomprehensible, he still urges wise and responsible behavior, because God is sovereign and will judge human behaviors.[47] So, while humans will never be able to understand what is good to the degree that God does, we "can discover what is good in a provisional sense. Some things are "better" than others."[48]

These proverbs explore what is good, and, initially, focus a great deal on death. It may seem like the Teacher is obsessed with death, but how we interpret his comments in these first verses should be influenced by how he opens the chapter talking about the value of a good name. How do we earn a good name for ourselves? Certainly not by never living, or by dying immediately. Rather, it is through our accomplishments, the good works we do, and the way we treat people that we earn a good name for ourselves, and it is at the end of life when one's reputation is established and can be evaluated as a whole.

This connects well to 7.8: the end of a thing is "better" in the sense that it is at the end when you can accurately evaluate something. It's easy to have big ideas or make grand claims about what you're going to do—ultimately though, it doesn't matter what you *plan* to do; it's whether or not you actually *carry it out* that matters. Just as you can only evaluate the

---

[47] Bland, 351.

[48] Ibid., 352.

worth of a project at its completion, you can only evaluate a life at its end. This is part of the wisdom that the Teacher offers.

DISCUSS: What do you think "sorrow is better than laughter" means?

First, it is important for us to realize that proverbs are not meant to be absolute statements; they are general truths. In light of this, the Teacher isn't saying that we should always be sorrowful and never laugh (after all, remember the seasons of life in Ecclesiastes 3). However, there is perhaps a warning here about pursuing a lifestyle based on thrills and pleasure that seeks to avoid any discomfort.

DISCUSS: What do you think "the heart of the wise is in the house of mourning" means?

This reflects a similar idea. In my experience, some of the wisest people I know are those who have experienced deep suffering. In my own life, it seems that my character has grown the most at times when the circumstances of my life have been most difficult. It is often the case that wisdom is developed through the crucible of hard times.

DISCUSS: What do you think "it is better for a man to hear the rebuke of the wise than to hear the song of fools" means?

Some of the best advice you will get in life will be advice you don't want to hear. It might be some wise person who is rebuking you for something you've done or is redirecting your energies in some way. It hurts to hear, but it is what you need to hear in the moment. What you *don't* need so much is a chorus of foolish "yes men" surrounding you who always tell you how great you are. That gives you a false sense of accomplishment, makes you prideful, and stifles personal growth.

The song of fools is further described in 7.6, where the Teacher compares it to the crackling of thorns under a pot. This is a metaphor that we can easily miss, but dry thorns were often used to help start a fire because they provided quick combustion. As they do so, they do not give off much heat, but the cause a lot of noise. Fools are the same way—they make a lot of noise, but they don't provide much substance with their many words.[49]

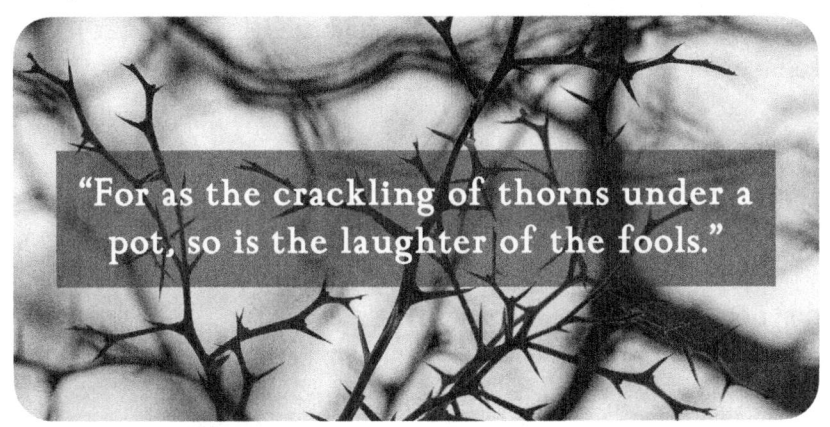

> "For as the crackling of thorns under a pot, so is the laughter of the fools."

Ecclesiastes 7.9-12

Be not quick in your spirit to become angry, for anger lodges in the heart of fools.

Say not, "Why were the former days better than these?" For it is not from wisdom that you ask this.

Wisdom is good with an inheritance, an advantage to those who see the sun.

For the protection of wisdom is like the protection of money, and the advantage of knowledge is that wisdom preserves the life of him who has it.

---

[49] Bland, 354.

Have you ever known someone who gets angry really easily? Sometimes we say that such a person has a "short fuse" because it doesn't take much to set them off. People that blow up with little provocation look foolish, and the Teacher warns us that we shouldn't be quick to get angry.

Have you ever heard people talk about the "good ol' days"? Usually when people say this, the implication is that everything used to be so much better than it is now. The Teacher seems to question the wisdom behind such statements, and in fact, if you remember his earlier statements about there being nothing new under the sun, it seems that he would argue that things are neither better nor worse: they are basically the same that they have always been.

Nevertheless, people say things like this all the time. For example, you might hear people talk about how bad things are now because a variety of sexual behaviors that the Bible condemns are now openly pushed as acceptable lifestyles. For those who care about what Scripture teaches, it can be tempting to say that our moral values are falling apart and that it would be nice to go back to the good ol' days!

But which good ol' days are we talking about? The 1950s, maybe? Back then, African Americans were openly denied basic civil rights. In many places and in many ways, they were basically treated as subhuman. What's so good about that? Or maybe we want to go back to the 1800s? Back then, childhood diseases were so prevalent that about one third of children died before reaching adulthood. Were *those* the good ol' days?

You get the idea. Sure, there are major problems with our society today, but that has always been true. Rather than spending our lives wishing that we could travel back in time to some perfect society that never actually existed, we would do better to try to apply God's wisdom to problems that exist today.

In 7.11-12, the Teacher offers some brief comments about the importance of wisdom. Remember, Ecclesiastes is wisdom literature, and the Teacher certainly sees value in developing wisdom; he just knows that wisdom, like the other aspects of life he has examined, has limitations: there are confusing parts of life that human wisdom cannot explain, and it doesn't have lasting significance.

Ecclesiastes 7.13-14

Consider the work of God: who can make straight what he has made crooked?

In the day of prosperity be joyful, and in the day of adversity consider: God has made the one as well as the other, so that man may not find out anything that will be after him.

Discuss: What do you think is the point of these verses?

It sounds similar to the idea of the different seasons from Ecclesiastes 3: there is a time for everything. That means there is a time for prosperity and a time for adversity.

Also, it reminds us of one of the consistent teachings of the Bible: **God is in control of this world.** I do not believe the Bible teaches that God specifically causes every single thing that happens, but He is in control. When things are going well in your life—when you are making good grades at school and getting along with your parents, and you find out the boy or girl you like likes you back—God is in control. But also, when things are *not* going so well—when you fail a history test, or your parents get divorced, or your grandfather is diagnosed with cancer, or your boyfriend or girlfriend dumps you—God is *still* in control. In the good times *and* in the bad times.

Go Deeper: The Good and Bad Times of Joseph

You are probably familiar with the story of Joseph, which is recorded in Genesis 37-50. Joseph experienced a lot of hardship in his life: he was hated by his brothers, sold into slavery, taken to live in a distant land, and imprisoned on false charges.

It would have been easy for Joseph to feel that God had abandoned him, or that He was not in control. And yet, God *was* in control, and He worked in difficult times in Joseph's life to bring about great things. Ultimately, Joseph rose to a place of prominence in Egypt, second only to Pharaoh, and in his high position, he was able to save his family from a horrible famine.

Like Joseph, we will experience difficult times in our lives, but God can use those difficult times to bring about good.

Ecclesiastes 7.15-18

In my vain life I have seen everything. There is a righteous man who perishes in his righteousness, and there is a wicked man who prolongs his life in his evildoing. Be not overly

> *righteous, and do not make yourself too wise. Why should you destroy yourself? Be not overly wicked, neither be a fool. Why should you die before your time? It is good that you should take hold of this, and from that withhold not your hand, for the one who fears God shall come out from both of them.*

DISCUSS: What do you think it means to not be "overly righteous" or "overly wicked"?

Admittedly, these are some tough verses, and scholars disagree about what the Teacher is trying to say here:[50]

- A traditional interpretation is that we shouldn't be too good or too bad, but rather somewhere in the middle: "everything in moderation." This doesn't fit well with the rest of Scripture, though, and seems to support a lukewarm faith where we just try to avoid doing terrible things and not worry about trying to be holy.
- Some interpret "righteous" in verse 16 to mean "self-righteous". So here, the basic idea is that we shouldn't think too highly of ourselves. Don't think you are so pure or so wise (when you're really not).
- A third possibility is that the Teacher is saying here that we should not trust in our own goodness to get us through life without trouble, because righteous living doesn't guarantee worldly blessing.

Whatever this means, exactly, Ecclesiastes 7.18 makes it clear that fearing God (an idea we already talked about in Ecclesiastes 5) is the proper response here. Compared to God, we are incredibly limited, and when we acknowledge that, we are reminded that God understands the elements of life that

---

[50] McMillion; Brown, 140-41; Bland, 357.

confound us and also that we can never be truly righteous on our own, no matter how obsessively we seek it. With this in mind, reverence toward God is the wise course of action.

Ecclesiastes 7.19-29

Wisdom gives strength to the wise man more than ten rulers who are in a city.

Surely there is not a righteous man on earth who does good and never sins.

Do not take to heart all the things that people say, lest you hear your servant cursing you. Your heart knows that many times you yourself have cursed others.

All this I have tested by wisdom. I said, "I will be wise," but it was far from me. That which has been is far off, and deep, very deep; who can find it out?

I turned my heart to know and to search out and to seek wisdom and the scheme of things, and to know the wickedness of folly and the foolishness that is madness. And I find something more bitter than death: the woman whose heart is snares and nets, and whose hands are fetters. He who pleases God escapes her, but the sinner is taken by her. Behold, this is what I found, says the Preacher, while adding one thing to another to find the scheme of things—which my soul has sought repeatedly, but I have not found. One man among a thousand I found, but a woman among all these I have not found. See, this alone I found, that God made man upright, but they have sought out many schemes.

Here we seem to have some additional proverbs. Earlier in Ecclesiastes the Teacher indicated that wisdom was *hebel*, but we see clearly here that the Teacher doesn't mean it is useless. There is still value in wisdom.

Ecclesiastes 7.21-22 offers helpful counsel: *"do not take to heart all the things that people say."* People will criticize us in life. When that happens, we should always consider what people are saying, but that doesn't mean we should always take it to heart. We shouldn't let the criticism of others (or the fear of others' criticism) control us. At the same time, we need to realize that we are often critical of others as well. It is hypocritical for us to get upset with others for being critical of us if we are frequently critical of others.

Ecclesiastes 7 ends with some extended thoughts on wisdom. Already, the Teacher has affirmed that wisdom is good, but that it is also *hebel*. Now, he also suggests that wisdom is very *rare*, and hard to achieve. Foolishness, on the other hand, is easily accessible.

The Teacher concludes the chapter with a summary of his investigations into humanity and wisdom: *"God made man upright, but they have sought out many schemes."* God has created order and balance in life, but rather than heeding God's design, humans have instead focused their attention in misguided ways. Indeed, this is one of the repeated themes we have seen in Ecclesiastes![51]

Live Deeply: Parental Perspective

The providence of God refers to the biblical teaching that God is in control of the universe and that He works behind the scenes to accomplish His purposes and guide and provide for His people.

---

[51] Bland, 362: "The irony in Ecclesiastes is that humans cannot straighten what God has twisted (1.15; 7.13); yet they twist what God has straightened out."

In the midst of our lives as things happen (sometimes bad or unpleasant things), it can be hard to see the hand of God at work or to feel like He is really in control; frequently God's providence is better seen in **hindsight**.

Have your students ask their parents (or grandparents if it is their grandparents who bring them to church): *"Looking back on your life, in what ways can you see how God has guided and taken care of you?"*

THE VALUE AND LIMITS OF WISDOM
ECCLESIASTES 8

The Point

Human wisdom is valuable, but it has its limitations.

Dive In: Wisdom as a Multi-Tool

To illustrate that something can be both valuable and limited, your students will try to accomplish a number of tasks using a multi-tool like the one pictured to the right.

Write different tasks on several slips of paper. Put these slips in a container and have your students take turns choosing a slip of paper and then attempting the task on their paper using the multi-tool. Some ideas are listed below; you will need to provide the multi-tool and some other materials as well.

[COMB YOUR HAIR]	[CUT A HEART OUT OF PAPER]	[UNSCREW A SCREW]
[HAMMER A NAIL]	[HOLD A PENCIL & WRITE WITH IT]	[MAKE A PHONE CALL]
[TIE YOUR SHOE]	[MAKE A SLEEVELESS T-SHIRT]	[CRACK OPEN A PECAN]
[PLAY A SONG]	[PICK A PIN UP OFF THE FLOOR]	[TELL WHAT TIME IT IS]

The tasks range from simple to impossible, and overall, show that the multi-tool is very useful, but can't do everything. Human wisdom is similar.

> ### Ecclesiastes 8.1-9
>
> *Who is like the wise? And who knows the interpretation of a thing?*
>
> *A man's wisdom makes his face shine, and the hardness of his face is changed.*
>
> *I say: Keep the king's command, because of God's oath to him. Be not hasty to go from his presence. Do not take your stand in an evil cause, for he does whatever he pleases. For the word of the king is supreme, and who may say to him, "What are you doing?" Whoever keeps a command will know no evil thing, and the wise heart will know the proper time and the just way. For there is a time and a way for everything, although man's trouble lies heavy on him. For he does not know what is to be, for who can tell him how it will be? No man has power to retain the spirit, or power over the day of death. There is no discharge from war, nor will wickedness deliver those who are given to it. All this I observed while applying my heart to all that is done under the sun, when man had power over man to his hurt.*

Rules, Rules, Rules

Wisdom has been a repeated topic throughout Ecclesiastes, and that theme continues in this chapter. It starts with a proverb that extols the value of wisdom (8.1), but will close with an acknowledgement of wisdom's limitations (8.17).[52]

Following the opening proverb, we have a discussion of how to be wise in relation to the king. The basic idea here is that it is wise to respect those who have power and authority over us and to obey the rules. While we do not live under a king today, we are still part of a society governed by rules that we have to obey.

DISCUSS: Are you a rule-follower or a rule-breaker?

I am basically a rule-follower. I get frustrated when people don't use their turn signals, or when they enter through the "exits" at Walmart. It is not hard to convince me to obey the rules; I do it naturally. Some people are not like that and naturally bristle when given rules to follow. Some rules are more important than others, but generally, it is important to follow the rules because without them, society breaks down. Foolish people disregard rules and try to live life according to their own rules.

In 8.5, the Teacher says that the person who follows the King's command will "know no evil thing", which although not an absolute truth, is generally true. A wise person will know to obey the king, and also will generally know the best course of action and how to behave.

This section closes with another reminder of the limitations of human wisdom and power, as the Teacher gives several examples of things that humans cannot control (cf. Ecclesiastes 1.18; 7.13-14).

Ecclesiastes 8.10-14

Then I saw the wicked buried. They used to go in and out of the holy place and were praised in the city where they

---

[52] Donald R. Glenn, "Mankind's Ignorance: Ecclesiastes 8:1-10:11," in *Reflecting with Solomon: Selected Studies on the Book of Ecclesiastes,* ed. Roy B. Zuck (Grand Rapids: Baker Books, 1994), 321.

had done such things. This also is vanity. Because the sentence against an evil deed is not executed speedily, the heart of the children of man is fully set to do evil. Though a sinner does evil a hundred times and prolongs his life, yet I know that it will be well with those who fear God, because they fear before Him. But it will not be well with the wicked, neither will he prolong his days like a shadow, because he does not fear before God. There is a vanity that takes place on earth, that there are righteous people to whom it happens according to the deeds of the wicked, and there are wicked people to whom it happens according to the deeds of the righteous. I said that this also is vanity.

DISCUSS: What is the Teacher saying in Ecclesiastes 8.11?

Unfortunately, a lot of times people do evil things and get away with it, and as a result are encouraged to *keep doing* evil things. The Teacher has observed this sad truth too, but he knows that ultimately, God is in control: in the end, God will take care of the righteous (those who fear Him) and punish the wicked (8.13).

And yet, the Teacher then goes on immediately to say that there are righteous people who appear to be punished as if they were wicked, and wicked people who seem to lead a blessed life as if they were righteous. And of course, this doesn't seem fair: we think that those who try to lead good lives that honor God should be blessed, while those who live selfish lives who continually do evil should be punished. Again, this is part of the incomprehensible *hebel* of life.

It is clear that the Teacher is feeling the tension between his convictions and his personal experiences: he believes that God will bless those who fear Him and punish those who are wicked (8.12), but he also knows there are exceptions to the rule, and that sometimes, bad things happen to good people while wicked people are blessed.

Go Deeper: Retribution Theology

Ecclesiastes 8.10-14 provides a good opportunity to discuss **Retribution Theology,** which is also sometimes called **Deuteronomic Theology** because it is described in some passages in Deuteronomy (Deuteronomy 11.26-28; 30.11-20). The basic idea is that when we do good, God blesses us, and when we do bad, He punishes us.

Is this a biblical idea that we should believe? Does God bless us when we are good and curse us when we are not?

Before answering those questions, we should first remember the context of Deuteronomy, where God is speaking specifically to the Israelites as they are about to enter the Promised Land to take possession of it. In this context, God is telling the Israelites what they need to do if they expect Him to support them in this massive task.

But even so, I think the Bible *does* teach this in a general sense. We do believe that, generally speaking, our good deeds produce good results while our sins produce negative consequences. The problem comes when we try to make this an absolute rule:

- Job's friends tried to get him to confess sin he hadn't committed because they couldn't believe he would suffer so much without having sinned.
- Jesus' disciples encounter the man born blind in John 9 and ask, "Who sinned for this man to be born blind? Was it him or his parents?" And Jesus says, "Neither."

This is not some sort of mechanical formula where we manipulate God into giving us good things by behaving ourselves. **As Christians, we love God and obey Him because we love Him, come what may.** We believe that this will result in the best life for us here, and certainly an eternal home with God, but we know that just because we try to live a good life doesn't mean that bad things will not happen to us.

Ecclesiastes 8.15

And I commend joy, for man has nothing better under the sun but to eat and drink and be joyful, for this will go with him in his toil through the days of his life that God has given him under the sun.

So, in light of the frustrating reality that sometimes the good are punished and the wicked are rewarded, what does the Teacher suggest? By now, it should be familiar advice: eat and drink and be joyful!

This is not the mindless pursuit of pleasure that the Teacher described in Ecclesiastes 2, and neither is it burying our heads in the sand and pretending that difficult and heartbreaking things don't occur. Instead, this advice stems from the Teacher's somber reflections about life: in the end, we cannot control or predict prosperity or adversity, so we should submit to God, realizing that He is in control, and enjoy those things with which He has blessed us.[53]

---

[53] Bland, 368.

Ecclesiastes 8.16-17

When I applied my heart to know wisdom, and to see the business that is done on earth, how neither day nor night do one's eyes see sleep, then I saw all the work of God, that man cannot find out the work that is done under the sun. However much man may toil in seeking, he will not find it out. Even though a wise man claims to know, he cannot find it out.

As we mentioned before, Ecclesiastes 8 begins by talking about how wisdom is good, but closes with a realization of the limits of wisdom. Ultimately, there are heights that human wisdom cannot reach. In our limited wisdom, we simply cannot understand why certain things happen, or exactly how God is governing the world.

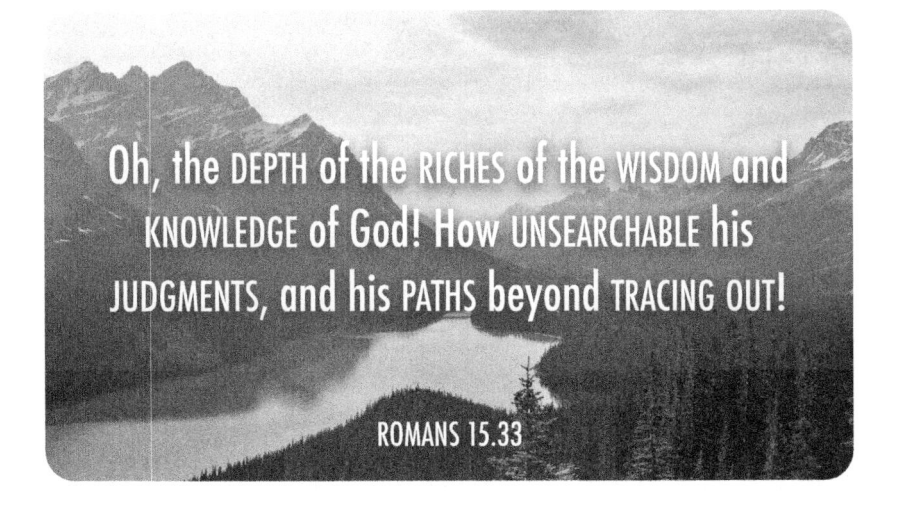

> Oh, the DEPTH of the RICHES of the WISDOM and KNOWLEDGE of God! How UNSEARCHABLE his JUDGMENTS, and his PATHS beyond TRACING OUT!
>
> ROMANS 15.33

Live Deeply: What Wisdom Can and Can't Do

Think of an older Christian from your congregation who you consider to be a wise person and invite him or her to come visit your class. Make sure to let your guest(s) know ahead of time what you will be asking them so they have time to reflect on their answers, but once you have them in class, ask them to:

(1) Share a story of a time when they made a wise decision that benefitted their life.

(2) Share a time when they experienced a difficult situation in life where human wisdom was insufficient to explain what had happened or why.

This will help to reinforce the idea that although human wisdom is beneficial and is worth developing, it still has its limitations.

DEATH IS COMING
ECCLESIASTES 9

The Point

Ecclesiastes teaches that death is a certainty for all of us, but that *when* it will come for each of us is very uncertain. These two realities should influence the way we live.

Dive In: Spending Our Last Days

To prepare your students for a discussion of Ecclesiastes 9, pass out sheets of paper and pencils and have them respond to the following questions (give them a couple of minutes to answer each one, and only ask them the second question after they have answered the first, etc.):

- If you knew that you had exactly 60 years left in your life, what would you do?
- If you knew that you had exactly 10 years left in your life, what would you do?
- If you knew that you had exactly 30 days left in your life, what would you do?

When all the students have had time to answer all three questions, get feedback from the class, one question at a time.

Likely, you will see that, with 60 years, the students' plans don't change much because 60 years seems like a long time, and would roughly be a natural lifespan for your students. With 10 years, students will feel a greater sense of urgency that might affect decisions about college, marriage, etc. With only 30 days left to live, students will almost certainly make some drastic decisions in order to make the most of their remaining time.

This is part of the message of Ecclesiastes 9: in view of the certainty of death and the *un*certainty of when it will occur, we should make the most of our lives.

> ### Ecclesiastes 9.1-6
> *But all this I laid to heart, examining it all, how the righteous and the wise and their deeds are in the hand of God. Whether it is love or hate, man does not know; both are before him.*
>
> *It is the same for all, since the same event happens to the righteous and the wicked, to the good and the evil, to the clean and the unclean, to him who sacrifices and him who does not sacrifice. As the good one is, so is the sinner, and he who swears is as he who shuns an oath. This is an evil in all that is done under the sun, that the same event happens to all. Also, the hearts of the children of man are full of evil, and madness is in their hearts while they live, and after that they go to the dead.*
>
> *But he who is joined with all the living has hope, for a living dog is better than a dead lion. For the living know that they will die, but the dead know nothing, and they have no more reward, for the memory of them is forgotten. Their love and*

> *their hate and their envy have already perished, and forever they have no more share in all that is done under the sun.*

Dead or Alive?

Ecclesiastes 9 begins with the Teacher reflecting back on what he has just been discussing: there are certain aspects of life that we cannot understand, we cannot predict either prosperity or adversity, and God is in control and sees the actions of the righteous and the wicked even when it seems like He doesn't (9.1).

Then he makes a transition and repeats an idea that we have heard already: no matter what we do in life, death awaits us all (cf. Ecclesiastes 2.12-17; 3.16-22). Reflecting on this, the Teacher argues that life is better than death. Although life comes with its share of problems, at least when we are alive, we can also enjoy life, look forward to good times, reflect back on good times, and have relationships. On the other hand, the dead know nothing and their passions have "perished". The living can work and accomplish projects and have relationships; the dead cannot take part in those things.

But wait, didn't the Teacher say earlier that it was better to be dead than alive (4.1-2), and now he says just the opposite?

Discuss: How do these two passages fit together?

Remember, the Teacher's earlier words were in the context of oppression. Those who are being severely oppressed may genuinely feel that death would be better than life. But in Ecclesiastes 9, the emphasis is that when a person is dead, he or she no longer has the opportunity to enjoy life. So really, what we have here is not a contradiction, but just the Teacher examining life and death from two different perspectives.[54]

> ## Go Deeper: Dogs and Lions
>
> In his discussion of how it is better to be alive than dead, in Ecclesiastes 9.4 the Teacher says, "...*a living dog is better than a dead lion.*"
>
> This might seem a little strange to us because in our culture we *like* dogs (we even call them "man's best friend") but in ancient Israel, dogs were a despised animal (1 Samuel 17.43), while lions were considered to be the mightiest of beasts (Proverbs 30.30).
>
> The idea here is that it is better to be alive and in a lowly position than to be dead and honored.[55]

Ecclesiastes 9.7-10

Go, eat your bread with joy, and drink your wine with a merry heart, for God has already approved what you do. Let your garments be always white. Let not oil be lacking on your head. Enjoy life with the wife whom you love, all the days of your vain life that he has given you under the sun, because that is your portion in life and in your toil at which you toil under the sun. Whatever your hand finds to do, do it with your might, for there is no work or thought or knowledge or wisdom in Sheol, to which you are going.

So, once we realize that life is better than death but also accept the fact that death comes for us all, what should we do?

---

[54] Glenn, 326.

[55] Ibid., 325.

Should we throw up our hands in despair knowing that death is unavoidable? Should we just cross our arms and sit in a chair waiting for death to claim us?

According to Ecclesiastes, no, not at all—we should enjoy life! Enjoy your food, wear your nice clothes, spend time with the people you love, and work with all of your might! Get as much out of life as you can! This is an idea the Teacher has presented before, but knowing that our lives are brief should encourage us to make the most of them.

Not only is this the best use of our limited lifespans, it's also what God *wants*: "these verses affirm that God does not simply *allow* humans to experience enjoyment, he *desires* them to experience it."[56]

> ### Ecclesiastes 9.11-12
> *Again I saw that under the sun the race is not to the swift, nor the battle to the strong, nor bread to the wise, nor riches to the intelligent, nor favor to those with knowledge, but time and chance happen to them all. For man does not know his time. Like fish that are taken in an evil net, and like birds that are caught in a snare, so the children of man are snared at an evil time, when it suddenly falls upon them.*

The idea of the uncertainty of life continues here. We should read 9.11 to say, "the race is not *always* to the swift, nor the battle *always* to the strong...." The point is that unexpected occurrences happen in life that cause things to turn out differently than we would have predicted. This may be exciting to us at sporting events (cheering for the underdog is fun), but in life, it can certainly be frustrating.

---

[56] Bland, 373.

Scholars and theologians debate about how much of what happens in our lives is controlled or caused by God, and how much is determined by random chance. I do not believe the mention of "time and chance" in 9.11 is referring specifically to that; rather, it is describing that from our limited human perspective, a lot happens to us that certainly *seems* random. We cannot predict what *will* happen to us and cannot explain much of what *does* happen. In that sense, we are like fish caught in a net or birds caught in a snare (9.12): we do not see what will occur to us ahead of time, and are not always able to do much about our circumstances as they develop.

From the Teacher's perspective, God is sovereign and ultimately in control, but that doesn't mean that we understand God's timetable for things or the bigger picture of the world that He sees, so much of life remains mysterious to us.[57]

Ecclesiastes 9.13-18

I have also seen this example of wisdom under the sun, and it seemed great to me. There was a little city with few men in it, and a great king came against it and besieged it, building great siege-works against it. But there was found in it a poor, wise man, and he by his wisdom delivered the city. Yet no one remembered that poor man. But I say that wisdom is better than might, though the poor man's wisdom is despised and his words are not heard. The words of the wise heard in quiet are better than the shouting of a ruler among fools. Wisdom is better than weapons of war, but one sinner destroys much good.

---

[57] Ibid., 375.

The topic of wisdom never seems to be far from the Teacher's mind, and he closes Ecclesiastes 9 with some thoughts on that topic, specifically by telling a story about a poor wise man who has used his wisdom to save a city from a great and powerful king.

Discuss: What was the poor wise man's reward for saving the city?

Nothing! No one remembered him! Still though, his wisdom did deliver the city, which supports the claim that wisdom is greater than might. Perhaps being wise won't make you famous or long-remembered, but it is an advantage to living a good life, and to helping those around you wade through the uncertainties of life.[58]

Live Deeply: A Discussion of Death

In American culture, we don't like to talk or think about death too much, and generally try to do all we can to avoid it. Repeatedly, though, the Teacher emphasizes that death *cannot* be avoided, and realizing this fact should influence the way we live.

Invite your students to share about people who meant a lot to them who have died. Be willing to share about people you love who have died as well. Emphasize that people die at all ages from many causes, but that (barring the return of Jesus), death will come for all of us. In light of this, we need to view life as a gift, and make the most of the time God gives us.

---

[58] Bland, 377: "Qoheleth's conclusion is that wisdom remains a reliable tool in the face of the uncertainties and misfortunes of life. Do not give up on wisdom."

THE POWER OF FOOLISHNESS
ECCLESIASTES 10

The Point

Foolish acts have great power for destruction.

Dive In: The Steve Bartman Incident[59]

It was Game 6 of the 2003 National League Championship Series, and the Chicago Cubs were just five outs away from winning their first National League Pennant since 1945. Chicago was beating the Florida Marlins 3-0 in the eighth inning when Marlins second baseman Luis Castillo hit a foul ball down the left field line. Cubs outfielder Moises Alou ran to catch the ball, but as several spectators reached out to catch the ball as well, one fan, Steve Bartman, deflected the ball and

---

[59] Wikipedia contributors, "Steve Bartman incident," *Wikipedia, The Free Encyclopedia*, http://en.wikipedia.org/w/index.php?title=Steve_Bartman_incident&oldid=638945389 (accessed September 14, 2021).

prevented Alou from making the catch. Instead of becoming the second out of the inning, Castillo was given another chance, drew a walk, and the Marlins went on to rally and score eight runs in the inning and ultimately win both the game and the series.

In the aftermath of the incident, Bartman had to be escorted from the stadium by security guards and even had to be placed under police protection for a while as he received death threats from angry Cubs fans who blamed him for ruining their team's chances at its first World Series appearance in almost 60 years.

Sadly, Bartman himself was a lifelong Cubs fan, and would never have intentionally done anything to hurt his favorite team, but in the moment, he made a foolish decision that had destructive consequences for his team and himself.

As we will see in this week's lesson, foolishness can be very powerful in that way.

Ecclesiastes 10.1-7

Dead flies make the perfumer's ointment give off a stench; so a little folly outweighs wisdom and honor.

A wise man's heart inclines him to the right, but a fool's heart to the left.

Even when the fool walks on the road, he lacks sense, and he says to everyone that he is a fool.

If the anger of the ruler rises against you, do not leave your place, for calmness will lay great offenses to rest.

There is an evil that I have seen under the sun, as it were an error proceeding from the ruler: folly is set in many high places, and the rich sit in a low place. I have seen slaves on horses, and princes walking on the ground like slaves.

The Vulnerability of Wisdom

As we saw in Ecclesiastes 7, at times the Teacher uses proverbs to get his point across, and we see this again in Ecclesiastes 10. In fact, for the most part, this entire chapter could be lifted up out of Ecclesiastes and placed in the book of Proverbs and you would never be able to tell the difference.

Ecclesiastes 10.1 goes really well with 9.18, which says, *"Wisdom is better than weapons of war, but one sinner destroys much good."* Here, the example of dead flies in perfume helps to illustrate the same point, that a little foolishness can outweigh a lot of wisdom. This is an important lesson to learn: a lifetime of wise decisions can be forever altered in a moment of foolishness! How often have well-known politicians or church leaders ruined their lives with well-publicized foolishness? Foolishness has great power for destruction. In this sense, wisdom is vulnerable to foolishness because it can be undone by it, but on the whole, the Teacher wants to emphasize that wisdom is still preferable; he never encourages foolishness.

In 10.5-7, the Teacher makes the point that even the rich and powerful are not immune to the destructive power of foolishness. A ruler makes unintentional mistakes and is brought low as a result, and a fool may take his place![60]

Ecclesiastes 10.8-15

He who digs a pit will fall into it, and a serpent will bite him who breaks through a wall.

---

[60] Graham S. Ogden, "Variations on the Theme of Wisdom's Strength and Vulnerability: Ecclesiastes 9:17-10:20," in *Reflecting with Solomon: Selected Studies on the Book of Ecclesiastes,* ed. Roy B. Zuck (Grand Rapids: Baker Books, 1994), 337.

He who quarries stones is hurt by them, and he who splits logs is endangered by them.

If the iron is blunt, and one does not sharpen the edge, he must use more strength, but wisdom helps one to succeed.

If the serpent bites before it is charmed, there is no advantage to the charmer.

The words of a wise man's mouth win him favor, but the lips of a fool consume him.

The beginning of the words of his mouth is foolishness, and the end of his talk is evil madness.

A fool multiplies words, though no man knows what is to be, and who can tell him what will be after him?

The toil of a fool wearies him, for he does not know the way to the city.

Continuing with the same theme, we have several proverbs about the dangers of foolishness, and the basic idea seems to be that even normal, routine tasks can become quite dangerous if we are not careful.

Discuss: For each of the proverbs given here, ask your students what they mean.

The first few proverbs seem to be related to the process of construction:[61]

- Digging a pit could be a part of preparing ground for building or a laying a foundation, but if not careful, the digger could injure himself by falling into the very pit he was digging.
- Breaking through a wall might be part of a demolition job. Ancient walls made of rocks or straw could have animals

---

[61] Cook, 109.

nesting inside of them, and the Teacher warns of the danger of carelessly breaking through a wall only to startle a snake and get bitten.

- Quarrying stone or cutting wood is a necessary part of collecting building materials, but if not careful, the person quarrying stone or cutting wood can be injured by them.
- Have you ever tried to cut wood with a dull axe, or drill a hole with a dull drill bit? It makes your work much harder and requires a lot more strength and effort. Being wise and making sure your tools are sharp ahead of time helps you to work smarter, not harder.

Moving away from the construction theme, the Teacher offers some additional proverbs:

- Snake charming is a neat trick and can be used to earn income, but if you are playing with the snake before it is charmed and it bites you, it doesn't matter how good you are at charming snakes! There is no advantage to that sort of foolishness.
- We've talked already about being careful in our speech (5.1-7), and now the Teacher offers some additional thoughts about the way we talk. Speaking wisely can earn respect from others, but speaking foolishly will destroy any respect that others have for us. Have you ever known a foolish person who "multiplies words"? Sometimes it is the people who talk the most who have the least to say.
- Finally, we have the idea that when foolish people work, they accomplish nothing because they work to no purpose.

Sometimes it is the people who TALK the MOST who have the LEAST to SAY.

Ecclesiastes 10.16-18

Woe to you, O land, when your king is a child, and your princes feast in the morning!

Happy are you, O land, when your king is the son of the nobility, and your princes feast at the proper time, for strength, and not for drunkenness!

Through sloth the roof sinks in, and through indolence the house leaks.

The chapter closes with some additional thoughts on wisdom, and the Teacher specifically talks some about kings.

DISCUSS: "Your king is a child, and your princes feast in the morning." What is 10.16 about?

Ecclesiastes 10.16-17 makes a comparison between two different situations. Here, describing the king as a "child" doesn't likely refer to a little kid, but, rather, indicates someone who is immature. Also, morning is not the proper time for feasting; morning is the time for taking care of business. The Teacher's point is that if your country is ruled by immature people who party at all hours of the day, you are in trouble. Instead, wise kings will feast at proper times and when they do, it will be characterized by what is appropriate for building up morale rather than drunkenness.

In the next verse, the Teacher continues with a similar line of thought. It is foolish to not take care of your house when the roof

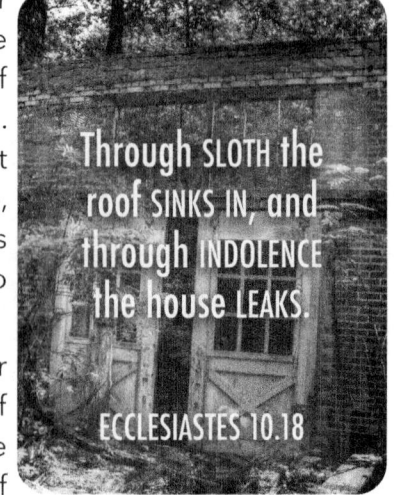

> Through SLOTH the roof SINKS IN, and through INDOLENCE the house LEAKS.
>
> ECCLESIASTES 10.18

106

starts to leak or you have a rotten floorboard.[62] If we are lazy and unwise, things will fall apart around us.

Go Deeper: "Child" Kings

Ecclesiastes 10.16 talks about the danger that can come "when your king is a child". The Hebrew word for "child" in this verse is *na'ar* (נַעַר), which is used over 300 times in the Old Testament and has a wide range of meaning (young man, servant, child, lad, etc.).

Na'ar is the word used to describe:

- A servant of Abraham's (Genesis 18.7)
- The 17-year old Joseph (Genesis 37.2)
- Baby Moses in his basket boat in the Nile River (Exodus 2.6)
- A young priest (Judges 17.12)
- Absalom when he was old enough to seize control in Jerusalem (2 Samuel 18.5)
- Jeroboam when he rose to a position of prominence (1 Kings 11.28)

Clearly, this word means more than the word "child" does in English.

In Ecclesiastes 10.16, the context does not suggest a small child so much as a young person who is lacking in experience and wisdom.

---

[62] Bland, 382, "The houses in Palestine had flat roofs. The walls were built of stone, and they used wooden beams as rafters for the roof. Without constant maintenance, the roofs were susceptible to leaking (see Prov. 27:15). A lazy person could bring about the demise of his whole house."

Ecclesiastes 10.19-20

Bread is made for laughter, and wine gladdens life, and money answers everything.

Even in your thoughts, do not curse the king, nor in your bedroom curse the rich, for a bird of the air will carry your voice, or some winged creature tell the matter.

Ecclesiastes 10.19 seems kind of random here, but that's not unusual in a list of proverbs. The book of Ecclesiastes has already discussed how God gives us good gifts (in this verse, food, laughter, wine, and money are mentioned) but we need to keep those things in proper perspective or they can become problematic.

Discuss: What is 10.20 talking about?

Here we have yet another reminder to be wise about what we say, and the Teacher basically says not to curse the King no matter what, because what you say might get out. We might not have a king today, but we always have people in authority over us (parents, teachers, coaches, bosses, elders, politicians, etc.), and this is good advice to remember.

This verse is probably the origin of the English saying "a little bird told me…." Have you ever noticed how secrets tend to come out, no matter how hard people try to keep them?

Really, in a general sense, this verse should remind us of the danger of talking about people behind their backs. We might say things about people in secret and try to be careful to make sure the people we tell will keep it to themselves, but a lot of times people are not trustworthy and the secret gets out. A lot of damage can come from this and relationships can be destroyed. We need to be very careful about what we say and to whom we say it, and the vast majority of the time, we probably would be better served to just keep our mouths shut: "if you can't say anything nice, don't say anything at all."

This last admonition from the Teacher is a fitting way to end the chapter: foolishness has great power for destruction.

> **Live Deeply: The Dumbest Thing You've Ever Done**
>
> You can end today's lesson with a humorous discussion by asking your students, "What is the dumbest thing you have ever done?" (that you don't mind sharing with the class!) To make the students feel more comfortable, begin by sharing a foolish decision or action from your own past, along with some of the negative consequences of that action or decision.
>
> You will likely get a wide array of responses, ranging from humorous or trivial actions to serious mistakes. Wrap up the discussion by emphasizing one of the major themes of this chapter: we need to be wise in the decisions we make, because foolishness has great power for destruction and negative consequences.

TAKE A CHANCE
ECCLESIASTES 11

The Point

Sometimes you have to be willing to take risks in order to succeed.

Dive In: A Risky Invention

Orville and Wilbur Wright owned a successful bicycle shop in Dayton, Ohio when they became interested in trying to solve "the flying problem"—achieving controlled, sustained flight in a powered, heavier-than-air aircraft.

Using mechanical skills they had gained from years of working with bicycles, the brothers experimented with gliders, motors, and flight controls, and began a series of tests in Kitty Hawk, North Carolina, where the windy conditions were ideal.

The financial risks of leaving their business behind to make cross-country trips were significant as were the physical risks—many aviation pioneers were killed in flight experiments, and both brothers were injured at different times.

Ultimately, though, the risks would pay off: the Wright Brothers

The Wright Brothers fly one of their gliders at Kitty Hawk, NC in 1902.

made their first flight on December 17, 1903, would go on to achieve wealth and fame because of their accomplishment, and aviation would change the world.

In the face of uncertainty—whether in the context of solving a seemingly insurmountable problem or simply in the day-to-day happenings of life—sometimes you have to take risks in order to succeed. This is an idea that the Teacher will focus on in Ecclesiastes 11.

Ecclesiastes 11.1-4

Cast your bread upon the waters, for you will find it after many days.

Give a portion to seven, or even to eight, for you know not what disaster may happen on earth.

If the clouds are full of rain, they empty themselves on the earth, and if a tree falls to the south or to the north, in the place where the tree falls, there it will lie.

He who observes the wind will not sow, and he who regards the clouds will not reap.

Business Advice?

Ecclesiastes 11 has a different theme than the previous chapter, but begins in a similar way: with proverbs.

Discuss: Ecclesiastes 11.1 is a well-known verse; have you heard it before? What does it mean?

Scholars have suggested two different possibilities. One is that the Teacher here is advocating generosity or hospitality.[63] Under this interpretation, the verses would mean something like, "if you are good and helpful to other people, they will be helpful to you in turn," and the Teacher suggests that this is a wise course of action because we do not know what bad circumstances might happen to us in life and when we will be in need of the generosity of others.

Another option is that the Teacher is actually offering investment advice.[64] In ancient times, doing business overseas was one type of investing that offered great potential for profit. Mediterranean port cities like Tyre and Sidon were popular places for importing and exporting, and it is possible that the reference to casting bread "upon the waters" and the return that would come "after many days" refers to this sort of overseas commerce and the lengthy time it would take. Of course, investing is risky, so if you want to invest wisely

ANCIENT TYRE

---

[63] Cook, 110; Bland, 386-88.

[64] David A. Hubbard, "Principles of Financial Investment: Ecclesiastes 11:1-8," in *Reflecting with Solomon: Selected Studies on the Book of Ecclesiastes,* ed. Roy B. Zuck (Grand Rapids: Baker Books, 1994), 342-44.

it is important to diversify, or spread your investments over several different industries, in order to protect yourself against risk. When unexpected things happen (crops fail, a merchant ship is seized by pirates, etc.), if your investments are diversified and spread out in several different areas (many waters), you will be better protected.[65]

Which option—generosity or investment advice—is the Teacher actually talking about here? Really, the two interpretations are not so different. In both, there is a sense of "investment", whether we are investing money in different **business ventures** in hopes of a good return, or investing in **relationships** by our generosity in hopes of a future return when we are in need.

> ### Go Deeper: Figurative Numbers
>
> In Hebrew, sometimes numbers refer to a specific quantity, while at other times, they are used metaphorically. For example, the number seven can carry the idea of "plenty" or "complete" in addition to referring to a specific amount of something.
>
> In Ecclesiastes 11.2, "seven or eight" does not refer to a literal number, but means something like "plenty and more than plenty." If we take this to be referring to investment advice, the idea is that we should invest a lot and spread our investments over several different areas.[66]

DISCUSS: What does 11.3-4 have to do with 11.1-2?

In 11.3-4, the Teacher discusses the weather and the importance of observing it and understanding what we see.

---

[65] Hubbard, 342.

[66] Ibid., 343.

The seasons are going to change and the rains are going to come according to God's timetable, and knowing when to plant, harvest, or travel depends upon the cycles of nature, not our own schedules. You don't want to sow seed on a windy day when the seed will be blown away, and neither do you want to harvest prematurely or too late based on ignorance of the climate. These verses perhaps strengthen the "investment" interpretation, and watching the weather would be similar to paying attention to the stock market today: we make better investments when we are informed about the climate.

At the same time, while farmers know the cycle of the seasons and what the general climate is like, they do not know exactly what will happen. If you spend all of your time watching the weather waiting for the perfect moment, you may end up so paralyzed that you don't sow seed at all (11.4), which would obviously be disastrous. Farming—and life in general—requires risk. It is possible to be too careful.[67]

> ### Ecclesiastes 11.5-6
> *As you do not know the way the spirit comes to the bones in the womb of a woman with child, so you do not know the work of God who makes everything.*
>
> *In the morning sow your seed, and at evening withhold not your hand, for you do not know which will prosper, this or that, or whether both alike will be good.*

Ecclesiastes 11.5 is a challenging verse to translate, and you may want to look at it in multiple translations. Instead of what the ESV gives above, the NASB says, *"Just as you do not know*

---

[67] Bland, 389, "The point is that there is a time to plant and a time to reap. However, do not be too meticulous in calculating the right time. Farming involves taking risks."

the path of the wind and how bones are formed in the womb of the pregnant woman..." The question is whether we are talking about one unknowable thing or two: is 11.5 discussing (1) the way the spirit comes to the bones in the womb, **or** is it discussing (1) the wind and (2) how bones grow in the womb? This confusion comes from the fact that the Hebrew word *ruach* (רוּחַ) can mean both "wind" and "spirit" (same with the Greek word *pneuma* (πνευμα) in the New Testament). As you can see, different translations handle Ecclesiastes 11.5 differently, but it is impossible to know for sure. Either way, the meaning is clear: while there are some things we can tell by observation (11.3-4), other things are simply unknowable for us: the work of God is ultimately mysterious and beyond our understanding.

But here comes the central meaning of the chapter: once we accept that there are things that are uncertain, the solution is not to throw up our hands in despair, but rather **to work diligently so that we can be as prepared for uncertainty as possible.** This is a Christian perspective as well: we should try to be good stewards of our resources and plan for the future as best as we can *while realizing* that we are not in control and that we shouldn't put our faith in our stuff.

In a real sense, Ecclesiastes 11 helps us to balance some of what the Teacher has said in earlier chapters. We might get the feeling that since we are not in control and do not know for sure what will happen, we should never take a chance on anything. But the Teacher says just the opposite: since you do not know what is going to happen, take a risk! If you don't try, you'll never accomplish anything. If you wait for the perfect opportunity, you'll never act. A wise person will do all the planning he or she can, and then take appropriate risks.[68]

---

[68] McMillion.

> **If you don't *try*, you'll never ACCOMPLISH ANYTHING.**

Ecclesiastes 11.7-10

Light is sweet, and it is pleasant for the eyes to see the sun.

So if a person lives many years, let him rejoice in them all; but let him remember that the days of darkness will be many. All that comes is vanity.

Rejoice, O young man, in your youth, and let your heart cheer you in the days of your youth. Walk in the ways of your heart and the sight of your eyes. But know that for all these things God will bring you into judgment.

Remove vexation from your heart, and put away pain from your body, for youth and the dawn of life are vanity.

When we are reminded of the fragility of life and how limited our understanding of it is, the Teacher (not surprisingly) suggests that our response should be to celebrate the "light" that we have and make the most of our lives.[69] Specifically, the Teacher realizes how short life is compared to death (*"the days of darkness will be many"*) and that we should make the most of the life we are given.[70]

In the United States, we live in a society that idolizes youth and

---

[69] Hubbard, 345.

[70] Murphy, 55.

tries to avoid death at all cost. We want to live for as long as we can, we try to avoid thinking about death, and we even avoid saying the word "death" and often use a euphemism like "passed away" instead of "died". For the Teacher, though, reflecting upon death helps us to live more fully in the present.[71] Life is *hebel*. It is brief and fleeting, so we should enjoy it.

And the same is true about youth: you will not always be young, so make the most of it while you are. Don't spend your time wishing you were older; enjoy your years of energy, health, and few responsibilities!

> **Live Deeply: Learning From Your (Church's) Past**
>
> Have one of the shepherds from your congregation come and share with your class about a time when your church took a great risk in order to better carry out God's mission (building a new building in order to be able to accommodate more people, planting a new congregation somewhere else, greatly raising the budget in order to support a new mission work, etc.).
>
> Taking risks can be scary, but in order to be obedient to God, sometimes we need to step out in faith and attempt great things for Him.

---

[71] Bland, 391.

THE END OF THE MATTER
ECCLESIASTES 12

The Point

Nothing is more important than living a life of obedient allegiance to God.

Dive In: How Would You Sum Up Your Life?

Sometimes people choose to have certain statements written on their tombstones as a sort of conclusion to their lives. It is a way of saying, "this is what mattered the most to me."

Cap Anson was Major League Baseball's first superstar. He played in the late 19th century, spent the majority of his career as a player/coach for the Chicago White Stockings, and was the first professional player to amass 3,000 hits. Anson's baseball accomplishments were so important to him that he left instructions that his tombstone read, "Here lies a man who batted .300."

As much as I like baseball (and you should too!), I think it is heartbreaking that Cap Anson would choose to sum up his entire life with a baseball statistic, and it reveals how skewed his perspective was.

In Ecclesiastes, the Teacher does not talk about what he wants on his tombstone, but he does end his book with a conclusion about what is most important in life. That's what this last lesson is about.

Ecclesiastes 12.1-8

Remember also your Creator in the days of your youth, before the evil days come and the years draw near of which you will say, "I have no pleasure in them"; before the sun and the light and the moon and the stars are darkened and the clouds return after the rain, in the day when the keepers of the house tremble, and the strong men are bent, and the grinders cease because they are few, and those who look through the windows are dimmed, and the doors on the street are shut—when the sound of the grinding is low, and one rises up at the sound of a bird, and all the daughters of song are brought low—they are afraid also of what is high, and terrors are in the way; the almond tree blossoms, the grasshopper drags itself along, and desire fails, because man is going to his eternal home, and the mourners go about the streets—before the silver cord is snapped, or the golden bowl is broken, or the pitcher is shattered at the fountain, or the wheel broken at the cistern, and the dust returns to the earth as it was, and the spirit returns to God who gave it. Vanity of vanities, says the Preacher; all is vanity.

The Coming of the Evil Days

Ecclesiastes 12 begins with an exhortation to remember our

Creator when we are still young, before the "evil days" come, and then goes on to describe what those evil days are like. "Evil days" may sound similar to the "days of darkness" that the Teacher discusses in Ecclesiastes 11.8, and they are related, but they are two distinct ideas. In 11.8, the Teacher was discussing death, and here he is referring to old age, the future time when one can no longer enjoy life in the same way.[72]

Following the first verse we have a series of statements that have traditionally been interpreted as a metaphor of human decline in old age and, eventually, death. There are other possibilities, but on the whole, the interpretation that this is an extended metaphor for human aging works well. Generally speaking, the Teacher seems to use illustrations from the decay of a house to refer to the decay of the human body.

Scholars disagree about the specific metaphors here and what they mean. Rather than go into every possible interpretation, I'll just provide some options so you can get a general idea of how the metaphor works.[73]

Discuss: To make this easier for your students to understand, you might want to make a chart on a dry erase board in your classroom. See if they can figure out how the different metaphors represent signs of aging.

- *"The sun and the light and the moon and the stars are darkened" (12.2).* **Interpretation:** This could refer to failing eyesight (everything becomes dimmer when you can't see), or in a more figurative sense, could refer to the

---

[72] George A. Barton, "Remember Thy Creator: Ecclesiastes 12.1-6," in *Reflecting with Solomon: Selected Studies on the Book of Ecclesiastes*, ed. Roy B. Zuck (Grand Rapids: Baker Books, 1994), 367; Bland, 392.

[73] Barton, 368-71, provides an excellent discussion of the extended metaphor on aging and lists several different interpretive possibilities along with scholars who argue for each. Generally, I have followed his conclusions here.

idea that as we get older, the brightness or enjoyment of life is dimmed (as it says in 12.1, there is "no pleasure" in the evil days).

- *"The keepers of the house tremble" (12.3)*. **Interpretation:** This begins the comparison of a decaying house or estate to the aging human body. The keepers would be the guards of a palace, and here probably is referring to our hands: you have likely noticed that older people frequently have shaky hands.
- *"The strong men are bent" (12.3)*. **Interpretation:** The strong men would be the masters of the house, and in the context of our bodies, could be talking about a stooped back, or legs that are less powerful than they once were.
- *"The grinders cease because they are few" (12.3)*. **Interpretation:** Grinding maids would grind flour in order to make bread. As parts of the body, this is likely a reference to teeth. In ancient times, it was very common for older people to have lost their teeth, and even today a lot of older people wear dentures.
- *"Those who look through the windows are dimmed" (12.3)*. **Interpretation:** This is probably again a reference to the dimming eyesight that comes with advanced age.
- *"Rising at the sound of a bird" (12.4)*. **Interpretation:** As people get older, it becomes increasingly difficult to sleep restfully throughout the night. This might refer to the tendency of older people to wake up as early as the birds.
- *"Daughters of song are brought low" (12.4)*. **Interpretation:** If the sound of singing is brought low (made quiet), this could be a reference to deafness.
- *"Afraid of a height"* and *"terror on the road" (12.5)*. **Interpretation:** This does not mean that old people are

bad drivers! It probably refers to the fact that when you are older, moving around from place to place becomes a physical struggle. Climbing up stairs or walking up a hill is very difficult when you are old, and in a time when travel was primarily done on foot, walking a lot when you are old could certainly become a terror, whereas it is something taken for granted by those who are younger.

- *"The almond tree blooms" (12.5).* **Interpretation:** Many almond trees bloom with beautiful white flowers, and this is possibly a reference to the way in which our hair turns gray and then white as we get older.

ALMOND TREE

- *"Desire fails"* or *"the caper-berry is ineffective" (NASB) (12.5).* **Interpretation:** Caper-berry was a plant used in the ancient world to increase sexual appetite, so the idea here is reaching a point in life when sexual desire is so diminished that the caper-berry is useless.

- *"Man is going to his eternal home" (12.5).* **Interpretation:** death.

- *"Silver cord is snapped," "the golden bowl is broken," "the pitcher is shattered," "the wheel is broken," "the dust returns to earth,"* and *"the spirit returns to God" (12.6-7).* **Interpretation:** The description of several things being broken or shattered refers to the death and decay of the body.

Then, in 12.8, we have again the familiar, *"vanity of vanities, all is vanity."* If you remember back to the beginning of our study of Ecclesiastes, we talked about the **inclusio** that is used in

Ecclesiastes 1.2 and 12.8. The repetition of the vanity of vanities line creates a *hebel* frame that influences how we read everything that comes in between those two verses. Life is vapor: it does not last, and remains mysterious and hard to figure out.[74]

Here we have the closing of the frame, and it fits very well with the extended metaphor on the fading and decaying nature of our bodies in 12.1-7.

Ecclesiastes 12.9-14

Besides being wise, the Preacher also taught the people knowledge, weighing and studying and arranging many proverbs with great care. The Preacher sought to find words of delight, and uprightly he wrote words of truth.

The words of the wise are like goads, and like nails firmly fixed are the collected sayings; they are given by one Shepherd. My son, beware of anything beyond these. Of making many books there is no end, and much study is a weariness of the flesh.

The end of the matter; all has been heard. Fear God and keep His commandments, for this is the whole duty of man. For God will bring every deed into judgment, with every secret thing, whether good or evil.

In a description of the Teacher in 12.9, it says that he spent his time *"arranging many proverbs with great care."* Many of the proverbs in the book of Proverbs are attributed to King Solomon, and 1 Kings 4.32 says that he spoke 3,000 proverbs. It is verses like 12.9 that lead people to conclude that Solomon

---

[74] See pages 23-24 for fuller discussion of the *hebel* frame.

wrote the book of Ecclesiastes as well, and perhaps he did.[75]

DISCUSS: What does it mean to say "the words of the wise are like goads"?

Goads are pointed sticks that are used to prod oxen or other plowing animals in the direction in which you want them to go. The Teacher is saying that sometimes wise words can motivate us to do what we need to do or prod us toward a certain course of action.

— PLOWING WITH A GOAD —

DISCUSS: How are the collected sayings like nails firmly fixed?

"Collected sayings" refers to wisdom, or perhaps the proverbs mentioned in 12.9, or maybe even the totality of Ecclesiastes itself. Either way, the Teacher indicates that truly wise guidance and words of wisdom are foundational. There are certain bits of wisdom that we have come to accept and they stick with us and influence our life choices.

Ecclesiastes 12.12 says, *"Of making many books there is no end, and much study is a weariness of the flesh."* Obviously, the Teacher values writing and study, but this brings to mind his earlier discussion on the value and limits of wisdom (8.1-9,16-17).

---

[75] See pages 12-15 for fuller discussion of the authorship of Ecclesiastes.

The more we know, the more we realize we don't know much. That is very wearying. Also, with much learning comes much vexation (1.16-18). Work and study are good things, but it is easy to get out of balance and overdo it.[76]

I would argue that 12.13 serves as the ultimate answer to the question posed at the beginning of Ecclesiastes: *What does man gain by all the toil at which he toils under the sun?* The Teacher spends a long time trying to answer this question, and he suggests over and over again that life is fleeting, that there is much we cannot understand, and that it is important to make the most of the time we have. But ultimately, life is about fearing God and keeping His commandments.[77]

The "end of the matter" is that we must live in an upright way, realizing that God is God and we are not, and remain obedient to Him. Our lives are short and often confusing, but we must make the most of them, and God will judge us for the way we use the time and opportunities we have been given. This is the meaning of life; this is what life is all about. This is how we can find true, lasting significance.

Go Deeper: Who Wrote the End of Ecclesiastes?

Many scholars believe that the Ecclesiastes ends with an appendix or epilogue written by a later editor (12.9-14), because in 12.9, there is a shift to a description of the Teacher in the third person and of the things he did during his life in the *past* tense. Does this mean a different person wrote the end of the book? There are at least three possibilities of what is happening here:

---

[76] Bland, 398.

[77] Bland, Ibid., "The idea is that fearing God and keeping his commands is the essence or substance of what humans are about."

(1) These closing lines are written by the same author as the rest of the book and reinforce the same basic points.[78] Now, in the epilogue, the author steps out of his Qoheleth persona and offers his conclusions.[79]

(2) These closing lines are, in fact, an addition by an editor who is trying to bring the many thoughts of the book to a conclusion and emphasize the main point. This editor could have been a contemporary of the Teacher, one of his students who helped to compose the book, or could have come along much later.[80]

(3) These closing lines are written by a later editor who *disliked* what the majority of the book said and is seeking to correct or reinterpret it.[81]

So, which of these options is best? These last verses reflect **continuity** with the rest of Ecclesiastes, not **contradiction**. Much of what is said here is also stated elsewhere: the limitations of wisdom (8.1-9,16-17), the importance of fearing God (5.7), and the judgment of God (3.17). It does not seem like the epilogue is trying to "correct" anything, so the third option should be rejected. Either of the others are possible, though.

DISCUSS: As you reflect back on our study of Ecclesiastes, what are some of the major ideas that stand out to you? Make a list of the different major themes that your students identify.

---

[78] Cook, 112-13.

[79] Bland, 396.

[80] BibleProject, "Ecclesiastes."

[81] Murphy, 55-56.

The Teacher makes many important points in Ecclesiastes, including:
- The importance of fearing God and keeping His commandments.
- *Hebel:* the brevity and mystery of life.
- The things people chase after—money, fame, relationships, accomplishments, etc.—lack lasting significance.
- *Carpe Diem:* enjoy life, make the most of the time and blessings God has given us.
- Human wisdom is valuable but has its limits.
- Work is a good thing but not the only thing; workaholism is bad.
- God is in control, even when it seems like He is not.
- There are different seasons in life, and we should appreciate the season we are in rather than wishing our lives away.

Live Deeply: Applying Ecclesiastes to our Lives

We don't just study the Bible for **information**, but also for **transformation:** it teaches us and changes us, helping us to be what God wants us to be.

Lead a class discussion and have every student respond to the following question: of the different major lessons and themes from the book of Ecclesiastes, which lesson did you need to hear the most? Why?

BIBLIOGRAPHY

Ecclesiastes Sources

Barton, George A. "Remember Thy Creator: Ecclesiastes 12.1-6." In *Reflecting with Solomon: Selected Studies on the Book of Ecclesiastes,* edited by Roy B. Zuck, 367-74. Grand Rapids, MI: Baker Books, 1994.

BibleProject. "Ecclesiastes." Directed by John Collins and Tim Mackie, June 10, 2016.

BibleProject. "The Book of Ecclesiastes: Wisdom Series." Directed by John Collins and Tim Mackie, August 17, 2016.

Bland, Dave L. *Proverbs, Ecclesiastes, & Song of Songs.* The College Press NIV Commentary. Joplin, MO: College Press Publishing Company, 2002.

Brown, William P. *Character In Crisis: A Fresh Approach to the Wisdom Literature of the Old Testament.* Grand Rapids, MI: Eerdmans, 1996.

Cook, F.C., ed. *Proverbs–Ezekiel*. The Bible Commentary. Grand Rapids, MI: Baker Book House, 1962.

Glenn, Donald R. "Mankind's Ignorance: Ecclesiastes 8:1-10:11." In *Reflecting with Solomon: Selected Studies on the Book of Ecclesiastes,* edited by Roy B. Zuck, 321-30. Grand Rapids, MI: Baker Books, 1994.

Hubbard, David A. "Principles of Financial Investment: Ecclesiastes 11:1-8." In *Reflecting with Solomon: Selected Studies on the Book of Ecclesiastes,* edited by Roy B. Zuck, 341-46. Grand Rapids, MI: Baker Books, 1994).

Landman, Chad. *Wisdom for Life: 6 Weeks in Ecclesiastes.* Hashtag Media, 2013.

McMillion, Phillip. *Wisdom Literature Class Lecture Notes.* Harding University Graduate School of Religion, Fall 2010.

Meek, Russell L. "The Meaning of הבל in Qohelet: An Intertextual Suggestion." In *The Words of the Wise Are like Goads: Engaging Qohelet in the 21st Century,* edited by Mark J. Boda, Tremper Longman III, and Cristian G. Rata, 241-56. Winona Lake, IN: Eisenbrauns, 2013.

Murphy, Roland E. *The Tree of Life: An Exploration of Biblical Wisdom Literature.* Grand Rapids, MI: Eerdmans, 2002.

Ogden, Graham S. "Variations on the Theme of Wisdom's Strength and Vulnerability: Ecclesiastes 9:17-10:20." In *Reflecting with Solomon: Selected Studies on the Book of Ecclesiastes,* edited by Roy B. Zuck, 331-40. Grand Rapids, MI: Baker Books, 1994.

Swindle, Devin. "What Dreams Are You Chasing?" In *Deeper Faith: 2014 Deeper Youth Conference*, edited by Luke Dockery and Jake Greer, 202-12. Fayetteville, AR: Deeper Youth Ministry, 2014.

Whybray, R.N. "Qoheleth, Preacher of Joy." *JSOT* 23 (1982): 87-98.

Other Sources

Gowensmith, Debbie, ed. *PointMaker: Object Lessons for Youth Ministry.* Loveland, CO: Group, 2000).

Jackson, Wayne. "What About Jephthah's Vow?" *Christian Courier,* https://www.christiancourier.com/articles/1081-what-about-jephthahs-vow (accessed December 14, 2014).

Schabner, Dean. "Americans Work More Than Anyone." *ABC News.com* (May 1, 2014), http://abcnews.go.com/US/story?id=93364 (accessed November 29, 2014).

Wikipedia contributors. "Steve Bartman Incident." *Wikipedia, The Free Encyclopedia.* http://en.wikipedia.org/w/index.php?title=Steve_Bartman_incident&oldid=638945389 (accessed September 14, 2021).

IMAGE CREDITS

Unless otherwise noted below, images for this book were either taken by the author, uncredited, in the public domain, or came from unsplash.com, a wonderful, totally free source for hi-resolution photographs.

Page 5: Lance McMichael, https://www.facebook.com/lance.mcmichael

Page 9: J. Smith for Visit Philadelphia, "The Thinker" at Philadelphia's Rodin Museum.

Page 11: Mike Izbicki, https://izbicki.me/img/scroll/scrolls-pile2.jpg

Page 13: "King Solomon in Old Age", woodcut by Gustave Doré

Page 17: http://consciouslifenews.com/wp-content/uploads/2011/12/washington_joye_illuminCC20_2.jpg

Page 33: From "Pictures of Money", http://picturesofmoney.org/pile-of-coins/

Page 41: Luke Dockery, http://goo.gl/FiV8iS; Movie poster from *Dead Poets Society*, directed by Peter Weir, Touchstone Pictures, 1989.

Page 49: Luke Dockery, http://goo.gl/0Dtb0o

Page 52: From "Historical Boys' Clothing", http://histclo.com/chron/ancient/egypt/clo/child/acecc-class.html

Page 57: From "Free Blog Help", http://freebloghelp.com/wp-content/uploads/2010/11/gold-gift.jpg

Page 61: "Jethro and Moses, as in Exodus 18", by James Tissot (1896-1900)

Page 67: From "Mr. Wallpaper.Com", http://www.mrwallpaper.com/wallpapers/beach-hammock.jpg; McKayla Mulroney photo from http://buzzfeed.com

Page 71: Apostle Paul mosaic, circa AD 494-519

Page 78: "I Am A Man, Sanitation Workers Strike, Memphis, Tennessee", by Ernest C. Withers (March 28, 1968)

Page 85: Stephen C. Potter, https://stevenintoronto.wordpress.com/2010/06/29/post-1-owl-at-mountsberg-conservatory/

Page 105: From "pngimg.com", http://pngimg.com/upload/snake_PNG4072.png

Page 106: Michael Schwarz and Grant King, The Chewaukla Bottling Factory in Hot Springs, Arkansas. See more cool photos of abandoned sites in Arkansas at http://www.abandonedar.com/

Page 113: From "Ancient Mesopotamia", http://joseph_berrigan.tripod.com/ancientbabylon/id34.html

Page 123: Amelia Saltsman, http://www.ameliasaltsman.com/happy-birthday-dear-trees/

Page 125: From J.W. McGarvey's *Lands of the Bible,* available online at http://www.biblestudyguide.org/geography/mcg-lob/LOB104.HTM

ABOUT THE AUTHOR

Luke Dockery has worked in youth ministry for over 15 years, and currently serves as the Youth In Family Minister of the Cloverdale Church of Christ in Searcy, AR. He loves teenagers and is devoted to helping them develop a mature and lasting faith in Jesus Christ.

Luke and his wife, Caroline, have three children: Kinsley, Seth, and Cora. A graduate of Harding University, Luke also received a Master of Divinity degree from Harding School of Theology.

In his free time, Luke enjoys spending time with his family, reading, and cheering for the Arkansas Razorbacks and Atlanta Braves.

TWITTER: @thedocfile | **FACEBOOK:** www.facebook.com/lukedockery
WEB: www.lukedockery.com | **INSTAGRAM:** instagram.com/thedocfile

Deeper Youth Ministry
—CULTIVATING LIFELONG DISCIPLES OF JESUS—

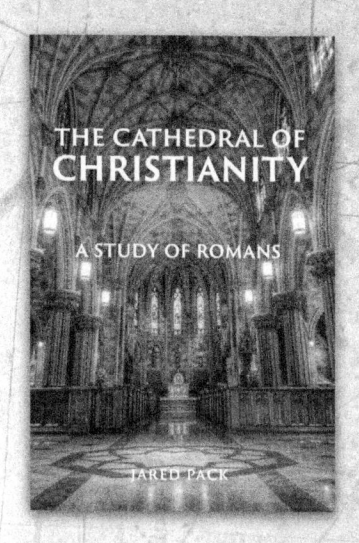

THE CATHEDRAL OF CHRISTIANITY
A STUDY OF ROMANS
JARED PACK

COUNTER CULTURE
A STUDY OF THE SERMON ON THE MOUNT
LUKE DOCKERY

WAR
A HANDBOOK FOR SPIRITUAL WARFARE
DM

NEXT MAN UP
A STUDY OF THE BOOK OF JOSHUA
JEREMY MYERS

CHECK OUT OTHER GREAT RESOURCES FROM
www.deeperyouthministry.com

Printed in Great Britain
by Amazon